Michal Bogin Feinberg

AF185621

Do not Disturb! I'm Drawing

A Journey of Self-Development Through Lines and Doodles.
Understanding Children's Drawings

Michal Bogin Feinberg

DO NOT DISTURB!
I'M DRAWING

A Journey of Self-Development Through Lines and Doodles.

Understanding Children's Drawings

ibidem
Verlag

Bibliografische Information der Deutschen Nationalbibliothek
Die Deutsche Nationalbibliothek verzeichnet diese Publikation in der Deutschen Nationalbibliografie; detaillierte bibliografische Daten sind im Internet über http://dnb.d-nb.de abrufbar.

Bibliographic information published by the Deutsche Nationalbibliothek
Die Deutsche Nationalbibliothek lists this publication in the Deutsche Nationalbibliografie; detailed bibliographic data are available in the Internet at http://dnb.d-nb.de.

First edition copyright © 2018; licensed from eBookPro Publishing (www.ebook-pro.com)

Translated from Hebrew by Roni Bogin

ISBN-13: 978-3-8382-1454-2
© *ibidem*-Verlag, Stuttgart 2021
Alle Rechte vorbehalten

Printed in the EU

CONTENTS

Introduction

How do we help the child to be creative and self-assured?

DO NOT DISTURB—I'm Drawing, deals with the development of drawing in children aged one and a half to six. It explains the meaning of this process, and describes how the parent (or any other observer) can encourage and influence throughout different development stages. The book will provide you with tools that will help you support your children to help **them** become more creative, joyful, communicative and self-assured.

The book provides us with answers to questions such as: When and how do the doodles and the lines first appear, and why is this so meaningful? When does the circle begin to "grow horns"? What is the meaning of the triangle? When does the child begin to mark a cross, and what's so special about that? **What emotional changes take place within the child during each of these graphic changes?**

From doodling to forming a figure—the progression in the child's drawings has a fixed order all around the world, and has a psychological and emotional logic to it. Understanding this order will provide the reader with meaningful insights about the child's inner, **emotional** world. The objective is to evoke curiosity and enthusiasm within you and to make you, the observer of your child's drawings much more exciting.

Understanding these different stages of emotional and motor development—and unraveling the "hidden secret" of the relationship between them—will help you to accept the child and their abilities at every given moment of his development. Observing the child's drawing with an accepting, appreciative, enthusiastic gaze will grant the child the validation of being understood, and strengthen his will to create. Who amongst us, children and adults alike, doesn't want to be understood and appreciated? Reading the book will also help you, (whether you are a parent, grandparent, therapist or teacher), to understand the child and encourage him to create and express himself. It will help you to add to the child enthusiasm, vitality, imagination and meaning, and thus reinforcing the child's self-esteem. As a result, you and the drawing child will be able to connect and communicate on a much deeper level.

* * *

I am an art therapist with many years experience in the field. Throughout the years, I have researched, taught and accumulated a significant amount of experience and knowledge about the development of children's drawing as a process that runs parallel to their emotional development. Nowadays, I use the experience and knowledge I've gained in order to help children, teens and adults.

I also teach and guide other art therapists. I've heard many therapists and teachers say, "Ah, I've already learnt a lot about the development of children's drawings. There are so many books on this subject."

"And do you remember anything?" I ask. "Not really," they answer with a smile.

In order to help you really internalize and remember the process of the development of children's drawings, I will give you a unique insight into the connection between the child's emotional and motor development through their drawings, one which I have developed throughout the years. Your manner of observing the drawing, accompanied by a real understanding of the connection between the child's motor and emotional development, is going to change and influence you after reading this book. This understanding will help you develop a more accepting, supportive, appreciative and enthusiastic observation (not necessarily in a verbal way). The way you observe is very important to the child's development. It increases his self-esteem, his love for creation, his curiosity and his motivation to keep and create, and also deepens the connection between the young creator and his observer.

During the process of writing this book, I have (more than once) imagined myself as a straight line aiming at a target. Even if the line occasionally bent, in the end it always returned to being straight. What helped it straighten was the enthusiasm of whoever read the book in the process of writing it, even at its early "doodling" stage. Such enthusiasm has encouraged me and evoked within me the need to continue to write. The strength to keep writing came from my desire to give away my knowledge and share my excitement over the lines, colors and shapes that teach us about ourselves in a unique and precise way.

Throughout this book, I will empathize the meaning, the complexity and the importance of the role of the parent or any other observer. I will help any observer to manage to express honest enthusiasm for the child's doodles. I will focus on the development of the child's drawings and explore the connection between the motor movement in his drawings and the meaningful emotional progression that occurs simultaneously.

I hope to demonstrate the importance of being **genuinely** impressed by the child's creative expression, starting from his early doodles. Any expression of approval and honest excitement in the moment of creation will encourage the child later on to develop autonomous and original thinking. The tendency to show the child how to draw a house or a figure, and even to occasionally correct him and teach him what is the "right" way of drawing, could damage the child's confidence and leave him with the constant need for guidance and direction from others who (allegedly) know better what to draw, and how.

An authentic expression of enthusiasm for the child's drawings, on the other hand, will strengthen him and encourage him to become an independent and original thinker as an adult. Therefore, it is essential that every person who raises a child, or works with him, will learn the stages of this development in children's drawing skills, for it is an important key for forming closeness with the child and for understanding him. In this book, I will share with you the secret of these stages.

My curiosity to this subject arose during my studies in psychology, when I discovered the books of the psychoanalyst, Frances Tustin. Tustin researched the world of the autistic child, as well as the autistic situation in general. To my surprise, I discovered that Tustin shows her enthusiasm for each coincidental cross in the therapy room that a child recognizes, even if it's only a part of a window frame. She interprets it as a sign of meaningful emotional development. This realization strengthened within me the understanding that there is a meaningful and fascinating connection between graphic shapes and a child's emotional development. Over time, I discovered another rich world of relationships between shapes and meanings. When I share these insights with my students, they all enthusiastically report a change that occurs in their approach toward doodling, and toward the early drawings of their own children and patients, and they all mention how much this new attitude influences the creativity of these children.

Later, I also found a resemblance between the process of development in children's drawing and the process of development in the drawings that were drawn by the adults with whom I work. It was interesting to discover that adults drawings demonstrate a similar, parallel relationship between the two processes of emotional and graphic development. That way, through the process of creation, many doodles and drawings of crosses and circles were created, enabling a person to redefine his own "self," to enhance it, to rearrange the process of his separation from the "other" and his connection to the "other," and also to improve the quality of the dialogue between his internal and external world.

I have designated the final pages of this book to the documentation of the children's drawings, so that, later on, they can serve as a reminder for your child of this particular process of transition from doodling to drawing a figure. Adults always like to know what has happened in the past, and how they were when they were little. These drawings are a testimony of an exciting and important process of progression. This can help your children—in the present and in the future—to have a better understanding of who they are, and will most likely contribute to the realization of how much they were, and still are, important to you.

Try to imagine this: in front of you is a drawing you drew when you were three years old. How do you feel when you look at it now? How does it feel to have an almost tangible grasp on a scrap of your own childhood? Once, I attended a school reunion to which someone brought a booklet of her classmates drawings, which had been given to her when she was sick. Even after all those years, the excitement this booklet brought about was huge, and many even went as far as taking photos of it to show their own kids. "It's an archeology of time" „... a journey into a time tunnel" "… a time capsule," were only a few of their reactions. It was as if this was a testimony of a childhood which no longer existed.

Here are a few examples from that booklet that caused so much interest at the school reunion:

To Nili—
A present to you from your First Grades class (written in the drawing)

It looks like children's drawing haven't changed much through the years, or even across decades. Isn't this incredible?

I wish you all an exciting and pleasant read filled with curiosity and creativity!

"Wisdom is the daughter of experience."

Leonardo Da Vinci

Chapter One

A look into art therapy

Art therapy is an instrument that aids us in expressing and communicating emotions. It combines the gaze of the distant observer, a view which represents insights and meanings—with the hand touching of the materials, which represents the sensory side sensuality and creativity. Through contact with concrete materials, such as different types of paints, clay, and various other materials, along with the presence of the therapist, a unique experience is created, one which enables the patient to express his own inner world using spontaneous images of the conscious and the subconscious.

Throughout the process of creation, the patient can express his early memories and pre-verbal experiences and put them into visual form – and, by doing so, he is able to make them more accessible and comprehensible. In this process, ambiguous thoughts can also become clearer. Creative work gives tangible shapes, colors and textures to feelings that have arisen and are now being revealed. During the process, it's as though these works of art are almost asked to be expressed, created and seen. There's a great deal of importance in the process of the expression itself, as well as to the visibility of the works and to their sharing. Later on, it's also possible to come up with additional interpretations from analysis and processing of the drawings. In art therapy, sometimes emphasis is given to the creative process rather than to words. At other times, the observation process combines words and becomes a conversation about the meaning of the drawing.

Each detail in the process of creation holds a meaning. A seven year-old girl who came to therapy in order to build up her self-esteem, has drawn during this process on a larger piece of paper, which she had chosen herself. Suddenly, while drawing, she said, "I now have a bigger voice!" Even an allegedly minor detail such as the size of the paper on which she chose to drew influenced her and reflected on her sense of confidence and happiness.

Art therapy places huge importance on observing the patient and listening to his associations. This creates a major opportunity, one in which the therapist and the patient observe the work together and then discuss its meaning, (only in cases when the patient is interested in doing so). Such observations and conversations are held with adults and children alike.

The meaning and interpretation given to the drawings are complex, and there is more than one right answer. If, for one patient, the color green can represent growth, for another it can represent fear or jealousy. If, for one patient, the sun can be aggressive, threatening and burning, to another it can be soft, warm and caressing. Sometimes the two different options can be applicable to the very same patient; it's possible—and advisable—to learn to live with opposite meanings that can occur in different situations.

Art therapy is very much about the reaction of the observer: an encouraging, validating observation, an observation which is devoid of any criticism or preaching, will influence the manner in which the child (or the adult) will draw. It will influence his ability to go on with the work or to abstain from working. Donald Winnicott writes about the great importance of this gaze, right from the beginning of infancy. He makes repeated observations on mothers and babies (in his book Playing and Reality) while asking: what does the baby see while looking into his mother's face? These observations allowed Winnicott to come up with the insight that, according to him, what the baby sees when he gazes into his mother's eyes is himself.

The gaze of the observer plays a great role in constructing the child's sense of self. Additionally, the therapist (or any other kind of observer) observing the drawing, reflects the drawing toddler's own sense of self, replicated in his drawing.

Heinz Kohut, the psychoanalyst and founder of the self psychology—a psychology that deals with the development of an ordinary sense of "self"—has emphasized in his writings (How Does Analysis Cure?) the child's need for adoration as well as his need to adore, as a force that contributes to leading a creative life from a young age. This is a basic need in the process of healthy narcissism development, which, in essence, is the child's ability to feel appreciated, valued and loved. The child needs the adoring and admiring reflection of the mother (when it is authentic).The authentic look of encouragement and joy on the observer's part is the part of the process that deals with constructing a sense of security and vitality within the child, so that he can grow and carry this confidence within him. The art therapist is skilled in observing in a manner which does not judge, but accepts and supports, as well as sowing enjoyment. Observing is a profound and complex process. When the observation benefits the patient during the creation process, his confidence will increase. Once he frees himself of thoughts such as, "This is what I needed (and wanted) to see," and of his own judgment, the observation becomes more open. It's at this point, that the patient begins to reveal more.

In this book, we will focus on a few basic principles of art therapy and will learn how to apply them onto our daily lives. We will learn and discover how every external change in the child's doodling process is parallel to his own emotional occurrences, and how these two processes influence one another. With this understanding, parents are able to perceive more, and in turn react with authenticity and enthusiasm from the very first lines that the child doodles. The child will perceive this appreciative, non-judgmental and accepting observation as a reflection of support, validation and enthusiasm for him and his work. This authentic enthusiasm will enable parents to enjoy the moment—the way the child is drawing right now, at his current stage of his development—instead of the way we would like to see him draw in the future, once he is able to draw a figure, a house or any other defined shape. The purpose of the child's drawing is not to satisfy the needs of the observer. The observing parent is welcome to join and accompany the child joyfully, hand in hand, travelling along the lines that are marked and created in the current moment.

This is a wonderful way for the parents to give their child a validation and make him feel appreciated and wanted. Therefore, the child will develop the motivation and ability to continue to create. These are valuable gifts for a meaningful life.

Chapter Two

"Scribbling," drawing and self-esteem—how do they relate?

When I asked an acquaintance for a drawing by her two and a half year old, her response was: "But these are only scribbles."

Is that so? Are scribbles really only scribbles?

The term "doodling," which is a more professional name for scribbling, carries a very important meaning. It represents the beginning of the creative process, expresses the child's own emotional development, and exposes their inner echoes, as the famous artist Wassily Kandinsky once said.

Doodling reflects situations in life. The more joyful and spontaneous the child's doodle, the more his ability to translate his feelings and his thoughts will increase, and the correlation between his inner and external worlds will grow accordingly. Doodling enables one to express a relationship with the environment. It's a vital form of expression and an incredible way to express emotions and the vitality and the richness of one's inner world, even before the appearance of words. If one can understand the meaning of a doodle, one can also appreciate and value every line in it. In constructing such appreciation, respect for the child also deepens and he feels more understood. That way, his self-esteem will be increased, he will feel freer to express himself, more valued for who and what he is, and he will have more courage to explore and experiment. That way, he can continue to doodle and draw joyfully, and lay the groundwork for his own uniqueness.

Why are visual imagery, doodles, drawing and an encouraging reaction so important?

They enable us to experiment and provide us with a space for us to explore the question: "Who am I?" They enable us to feel happiness, fun, satisfaction and calmness. Through this process, the child is granted with a space where he can get to know his own abilities.

Drawings and doodles also allow us to express ourselves more freely, which gives us courage and confidence, and also an ability to rely on ourselves and build an independent identity. These are tools which contribute to the construction of high self-esteem.

In addition to that, doodling and drawing also open up a new, alternative space where we can grab a seat, observe and also be observed. It's a place for us to express a variety of emotions; it's a bridge between the internal and external world; a tool which helps us to know and enrich our world of imagination as well as our real, tangible world.

Drawing and doodling help us to improve the way we plan and organize, and also to improve our ability to persist and dedicate ourselves to one thing. They are wonderful tools which help us develop our ability to imagine and symbolize. They also improve the skills of expression and interpersonal communication, which is often a means of bringing parents (and other important figures in the child's life) closer together with their children.

So, to the mothers who ask me, "Why doesn't my child draw?" or "Why's the paper on which he's supposed to draw in kindergarten always blank?" I usually explain:

Doodling and drawing are processes that can occur naturally and intuitively in any place and in any way. The toddler may doodle on the beach or during playtime, or while eating porridge.

Children who "do not draw" have come to me for therapy more than once, and have begun to love and enjoy drawing. How did this happen? I didn't do much. I "simply" listened to the drawing with no expectations and with great enjoyment in what the child brought. And it worked. The child began to draw happily and lovingly.

So why do children sometimes abstain from drawing on paper? Expectations. Drawing on paper might promote a greater expectation for results, expectations that the child receives from his environment, and influence his ability to produce results on the grounds of "performance anxiety." It's not unlikely that the same child, if he'd grown up in the jungle, or in any other place where the expectation for immediate results had not spoiled his toddler's natural tendencies, then he would have been able to draw freely.

It is true that not all children are equal in their ability to draw and control their doodle. Children may demonstrate greater or lesser control, and some may even have development disorders, motor problems or attention deficit disorders (such disorders should be looked into), but what about love for the play itself? For creating for the sake of pure fun? In this book, we won't deal with the differences in children's abilities, but rather with the love for the play and the possibilities of creation, which are so important for the development of each and every one of us. Much like Erno Stern ,the pioneer of creative education says; the act of painting is an integral part of

Chapter Three

The drawing, the "me" and the soul of the child: changing and evolving together

In order to deepen the understanding and interest in children's drawings, starting from the doodling stage, I will describe the development in children's drawings and how this process is parallel to the child's emotional growth. I will also focus on the changes which occur in drawings of children aged approximately one-and-a-half, once the child starts to draw shapes. I will try to explain the huge influence these two parallel processes have on the child's emotional world.

Motor development, starting from the doodles, reflects the child's process of emotional development, during which a sense of consistency, method and cohesion is formed within him – one which binds and collects his different experiences together. A sense of awareness of the existence of a separate self also begins to form within him, along with the construction of his own identity.

The French author, George Perec, wrote in his book, Species of Spaces and Other Pieces, that in order to transfer from the personal realm of the self, into the public realm that pertains to the "other," one is in need of a password, and simply cannot slide from one sphere to another. In order to do so, according to Perec, he would need to first cross the threshold, to communicate.

The doodling progresses into drawings with clear shapes that can be perceived as a "portrayal of one's soul", an illustration portraying the emotional development that is occurring simultaneously.

In the beginning of the process, the act is instinctive and it involves several different senses. There are many different undefined directions in the first doodles. It appears that the child draws as a way of exploring and playing solely for himself. As his drawings progress, his shapes become clearer and clearer—with separate lines for example—and demonstrate the construction of his identity as a separate self, and forming stability. The formation of a "sense of self" as a process of letting go of the illusion of the child's oneness with his mother is also a formation of the idea that there exists such a thing as an "other."

Later on, with the existence of such an "other," the child realizes rather quickly that he is being observed, and the way in which he is being observed will begin to have an influence on him. The relationship with the "other" progresses and begins to influence the child's awareness to the presence of an "other." The drawing child learns that the "other" responds, and those responses begin to be meaningful to him and influence the way in which he draws. Once he has this awareness, he begins to have the need to please the observer. The child begins to perceive his own self according to the reaction of the other.

Jacques Lacan, one of the greatest psychoanalysts, has written a lot about the role of the gaze and its meaning to the process of the infant's growth. This stage of development of awareness to the existence of a "self" and of an "other", was named by Lacan "the mirror stage." According to Lacan, this is a process in which the "me" begins to form out of the image and the reflection of the "other" within him.

The journey of finding the "real self" and the attempt to estimate how much the other is embedded within, along with the extent of the influence of the other – begins only now. The dialogue between the child obeying the expectations of an "other," and the child obeying his own needs and desires, will go on for many years to follow. From what we can gather, attention and awareness given to the manner of observing, along with a response which encourages the child to create in an honest and a carefree way, are very important in keeping the child's "self," his confidence, and the feeling that he is loved for who he is. This response will have an influence on his happiness and creativity.

During the following chapters, I will describe in more depth and detail the movements and the development of the child, which occur simultaneously in his drawings and in his inner emotional world.

Chapter Four

From the doodle to the circle and on to drawing a figure

A | Doodling the beginning: ages one to three

The doodling stage begins at approximately the age of one, as a part of a fun and spontaneous game. The toddler, out of a basic and natural need, loves to move, explore and experiment. According to Prof. Ben Ami Scharfstein, a renowned researcher in the fields of Philosophy and History of Arts, the doodle, since it is not a particular thing, could be just about anything. Once doodling, the child, too, can become anything he desires, and that is why any doodle can bring with it a wonderful experience. Doodles at this stage are simply traces left by the child's joy from the light movements of his own hands. It's a part of the child's natural need to discover and explore his surroundings.

That way, the marked lines begin to walk, much like the child moving around his surroundings—searching for a direction. The doodle represents the child's vitality and his need for expression and movement. At the beginning of the doodling process, the child still doesn't grasp the connection between what the eye sees and what the hand marks. The lines drawn on the paper are scattered in every direction in an arbitrary manner, while the understanding and perception of space still do not exist. The lines are wavy, spiral, entangled within one another with no apparent method or order. The child lives the movement and is being led by it and many times can continue beyond the paper's limits. The child senses that something is being created and the joy he produces out of it is great and intriguing. At this stage, the doodle still doesn't serve as a representative and communicative language. The child, the drawing hand and the paper function as one entity in the child's experiential perception. The paper does not function as an entity that is separate from him. Perhaps it's similar to the baby's perception of the mother as part of himself, and not yet as a separate being—according to his perception.

During the primal doodling stage, the most significant experience for the child is that of creating a mark and leaving it on the paper, while the result holds no particular meaning. The main thing for the child is the experience itself, the feeling that he is leaving some kind of impression on the world. This experience generates within him the motivation to keep searching, exploring and discovering. A child who comes across a pencil that doesn't write will most likely stop drawing because the marking experience will be lacking.

The mark on the paper demonstrates the child that the act he is performing is, in itself, influential, and that something of his own self has been imprinted on an "other" and is now representing him to the outer world. It's an expression of his own existence. Doodling serves as an important testimony to the toddler's expression of complexity and vitality, and to the fact that he has a lot to say to the world, even before he can form words. Perhaps it's much like the sounds and the mumbling that are typical to children of that age, that are later followed by whole words with meaning and symbolism. Similarly, with the doodle, an experience of an inner world begins to burst out and leave its mark on the outside world.

Primary doodle: lines are wavy, intertwined.

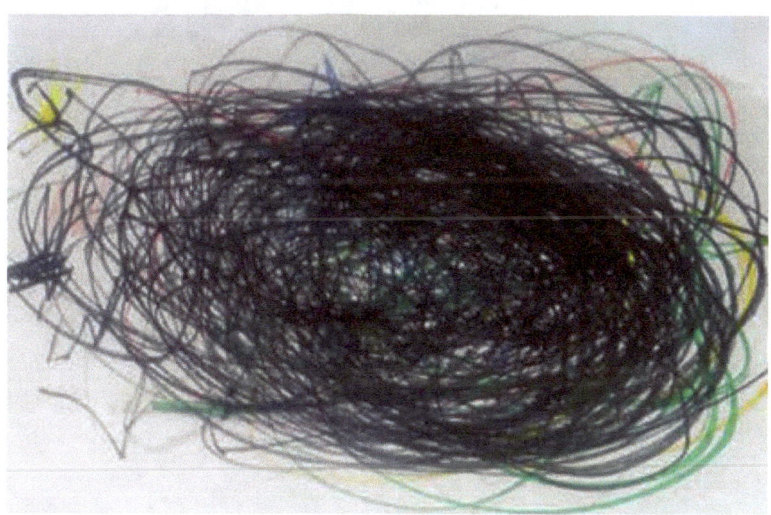

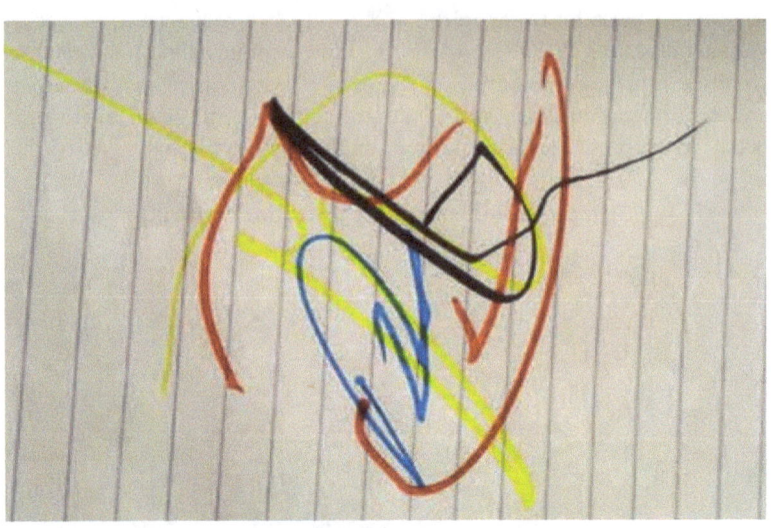

The lines continue to separate

Over time, the child discovers that every movement he makes using pencil or paint is not coincidental, but rather that he influences the different marks on the paper. Changing the movement will manufacture different marks. The child enjoys the repetition of this experience as well as the renewal and the surprise that it contains, and through this experience he begins to evolve.

Around the age of two to three, the child's ability to express himself improves, and he learns that he's able to influence and control the lines on the paper using his movements. He begins to observe what's happening with greater attention, and his ability to plan increases. Out of the first wavy, scattered and intertwined lines, which were typical of the first stages of his doodling, much more measured and organized lines will now start to form—straighter, more condensed lines, ones which require more complex motor and emotional abilities.

At this stage, vertical and horizontal lines begin to form, and the order in which they appear in the child's drawings is not coincidental. Normally, the vertical lines will appear first, and they will be followed by horizontal lines, representing the child facing outwards, and are typical of a more advanced stage of development.

Occasionally, at this stage, the child will begin to name his doodles and indicate what the object is, even though the lines drawn do not resemble what the object looks like in real life. The name the child chooses is derived out of his own experience and his association of the movement of doodling, as a flickering of the moment rather than a response to being asked what the drawn object is.

A line can represent a road, a house or a figure, much like the games of "pretend" which are very typical of children around that age, when a box can become a telephone, a house or a car. At this stage, the child's abilities to imagine and to use symbolism within games and in drawings are developing.

Once the child begins to speak and name objects, there's a great temptation to ask, "What did you draw?"

However, it's better to refrain from doing that. It might block the child. The child needs to take things at his own pace, so he can continue to enjoy the process in a way that precisely fits his development.

Over time, the child's manner of organizing and controlling his own body movements in general, particularly while doodling, grows and evolves. The line he makes is no longer only a sensual and kinetic experience; it's now a line that begins to be accurate and knows where it's going. We can look at it as the first signs of determination and assertiveness. These are, indeed, big words, but everything really does start here.

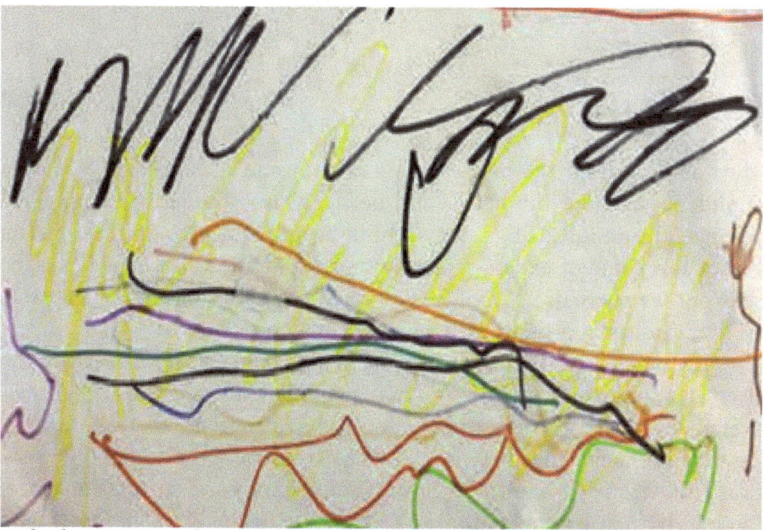

The beginning of control and planning in the doodle; horizontal and vertical lines appear.

It's important to mention that, even though the doodles are derived out of a similar developmental structure, style may vary from one child to another: the intensity of the line, the manner of filling the page, occupying more or less space on the paper, the scattering and the focusing, the energy invested in pressing on the paint, the stability—and more. All these possibilities are right and appropriate.

Different ways of doodling can teach us about the child's mood or temperament on that particular day and in general. We can learn when he's more withdrawn or introverted, and when he's more impulsive and free. Different styles can appear in the very same drawing. The movement of the lines is an indicator of the energy and the changing pace of his body and soul. Every doodle has its own unique character, just as every person or child does. This uniqueness is the source of the authenticity and the vitality of his work. Try to copy a child's doodle. It's very hard to do, isn't it?

Below, you can see doodles in different styles:

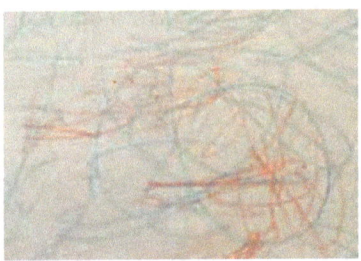 

Scattered upon the page   **Focused**

The doodling child will move his hand lightly and the lines will flow with confidence without the need—and perhaps also without the ability—to translate the doodle using rational thinking and interpretation. He's doing it as a fun game of experimentation and exploration. He creates for the sake of the experience of that very moment, not for a result, a purpose or an idea, nor for appreciation or acknowledgement.

How wonderful it is to be able to create in such a manner, out of the need to explore, and for the momentary joy, without criticism, without prejudice or defensiveness. It's a one-of-a-kind experience that's almost impossible to repeat, an experience which gets lost very quickly in our emotional repertoire as human beings. Painters, sculptors, writers and poets (and perhaps also people of other professions) try to recreate this feeling of primal vitality, and to connect to the present moment with this sort of intensity.

Tamar Doborovski, an abstract painter, describes the act of creation and primality:

"This series of drawings was created using a fast, automatic movement. On a wet surface, using a knife engraving marks, lines and paths were formed. A paint stain with a sketched answer upon it. A colorful surface and a reaction of the hand movement. A musical rhythm and a flow have appeared. Such occurrences, during creation, have brought with them a primal sense of coming into being. The disorder becomes ordered, the chaos forms into shape. New worlds were made during this creation.

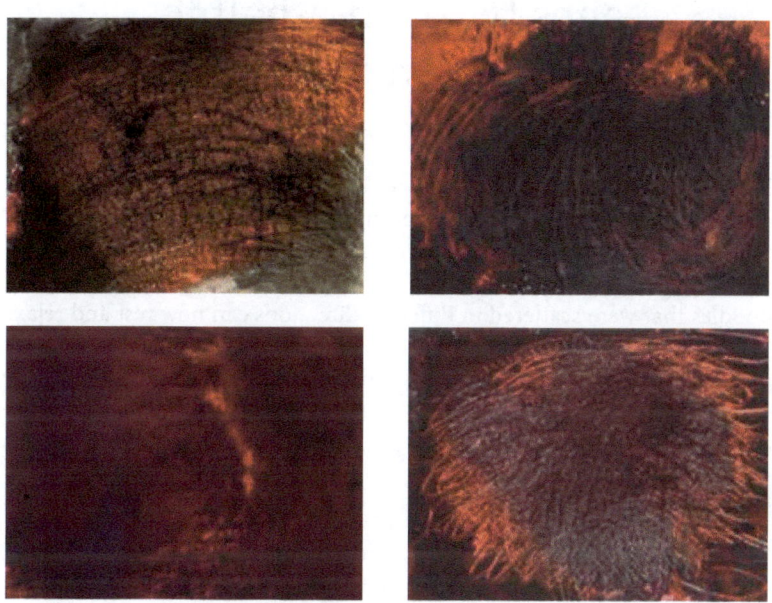

Tamar Doborovski, the series of paintings "Creation" 2004–2005, acrylic on paper, 56-57 cm

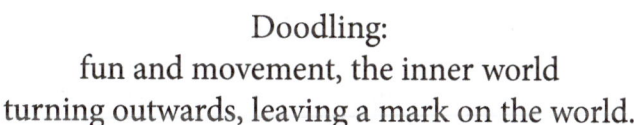

Doodling:
fun and movement, the inner world
turning outwards, leaving a mark on the world.

B | A circle is born: ages two-and-a-half to three-and-a-half

How is a circle born? Out of the doodling "cocoon," a cursive line is discovered, one whose end and beginning meet to form a whole circle. In that manner, all the "edges of life" gather and render into a pleasant and protective circle, known by some as "the mother of all shapes." All the other doodles that were scattered in different directions can now rest and relax. "The circle is an expression of this feeling of everlasting containment and satisfaction," Frances Tustin, the psychoanalyst said.

Marking a circle requires certain motor, cognitive and emotional abilities that are more evolved and controlled. It is the drawing of one straight line as opposed to many little lines and dots, and therefore requires the ability to estimate space. The process is that of moving from an abstract movement into a defined movement. Marking a circle is the beginning of the creation of a real shape, one which is framed and has a meaning to it, a shape that is recognized by the imagination as a symbol with an official name: "the circle."

The circle is born out of the doodle:

More examples of the creation of circles:

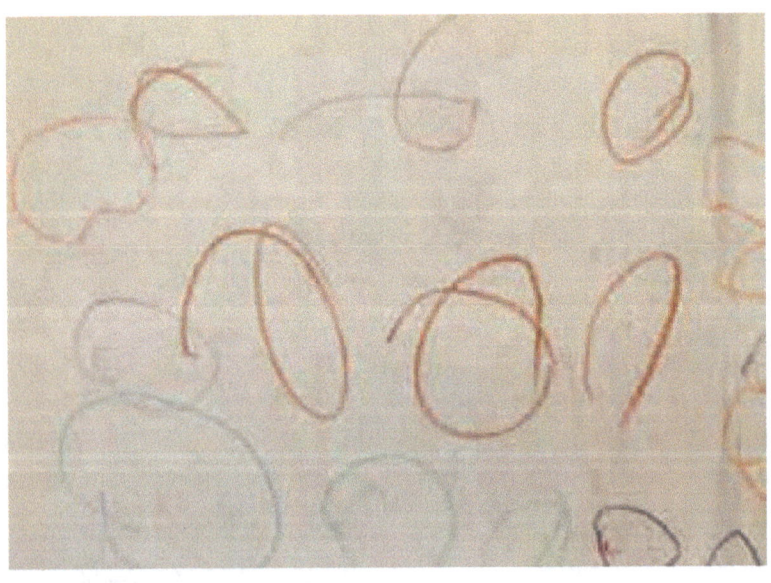

The process of the formation of a circle is a type of birth that can bring a lot of excitement with it. It's a process that isn't obvious. The circle is a meaningful shape, one that can serve as a symbol and a connection between the world of imagination and the real world. It reflects the emotional and physical development of the child.

The birth of the circle out of the doodle resembles the birth of the "self" that unravels out of the doodle. The circle represents the demarcation of the center of the "self" and the formation of an inner world. Focusing inward enables the child to develop thinking and creating ability.

Around the same time that the circle is formed, the child's communicative expression and his language also begin to develop. The child begins to say "me." Drawing a circle, pronouncing the word "me," and having a sense of a "me" all begin to develop around the same time.

This way, when the child discovers the "me," he also begins to discover there is an "other" out there—the world of the "not-me." Inside the circle is the "me," and everything outside of it (perhaps other circles) represents the "other," the separateness. He begins to understand that there is a dialogue between the "me" and the "other," and he now attempts to fit his own circle, that of the "me," into that of the other– the "not-me." Experimenting with one's circles and with the circles of "others" then occurs and finds its expression in games, drawings, dances, and social relationships.

Drawing a circle, an act which requires planning, demonstrates the thought and imaginative abilities that have expanded within the child. It's a graphic representation of his own thinking space, his ability to symbolize and imagine. In addition, different games of "pretend" with various objects and roleplay continue to evolve during this stage. It is the beginning of the transition from being a toddler to being a mature child. Allow the circle to be born when the time is right and appropriate for the child. There's no need to rush it. The circle will come!

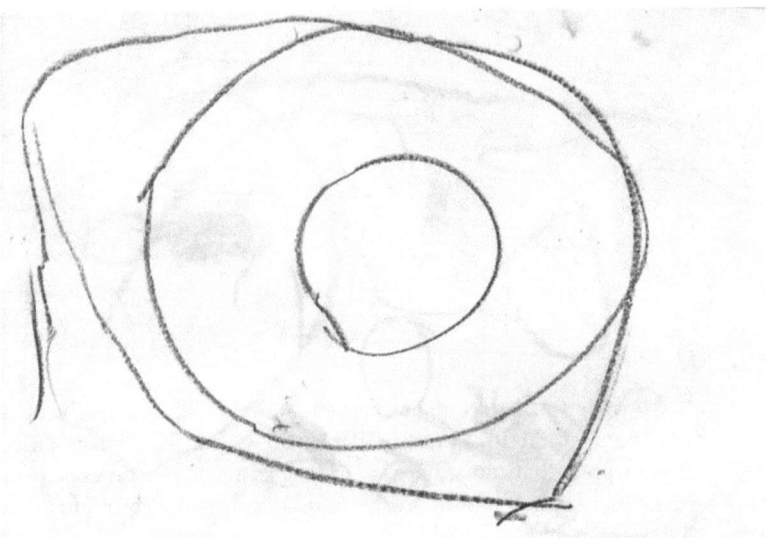

The circle represents the "me" in light of the "other."

We can also see the deep and meaningful aspect the circle has in the child's development if we take a look at the history of the world. Engravings of spirals and circles have been found in the caves of prehistoric man. Is there, hence, a parallel between the beginning of culture and the beginning of the toddler's emotional and motor development?

There's a traditional Jewish tale about Choni the "Circle-drawer", who lived in the first century BCE. Choni the "Circle-drawer", was asked to bring rain during a drought. He surrounded himself with a circle and prayed in it, in order to be protected by the circle he'd marked. The prayer from the center of the circle brought, according to the tale, the awaited rain. The circle seemingly constituted for him a space which was protective, binding and whole, a deep place for concentrating on one's inner strength, a place which is separate—even if only in a symbolic manner—from the outer world. The circle represented the good path, the path of persistence and concentration and, as a result, the skies were able to open up.

In the Indian sub-continent, the circle holds a very important meaning. Its name in Sanskrit is "mandala" (manda—essence, la—container).The mandala is described as a "sacred circle" and in Indian culture represents the observation of one's inner center and the bonding with the "me;" it symbolizes spirituality, infinity, the universe and the human soul. In most mandalas, there is a significant center from which contexts are drawn, which represent, in their cultural and religious perception, enlightenment. The Tibetans draw mandalas as part of the process of learning, as a curative and meditative act.

Karl Gustav Jung (1875-1961), the Swiss psychoanalyst, has empathized the spiritual aspects of therapy and was deeply influenced by Indian culture. Inspired by it, he used the mandala as a source of emotional therapy, both for himself and for his patients. He discovered that drawing circles and coloring them relaxes and focuses the patient, in a "sort of renewed organization around a center," and that reflects the emotional state and the person's "self" on that particular day. Jung drew a different mandala each day.

The circle also has an important meaning in Japanese culture. In Japan, the circle is called ensu. Ensu drawings were drawn in calligraphy using a special brush that represents enlightenment, empty space and infinity. Zen students draw the ensu as a daily meditative practice. The calligraphy which appears here, One Monkpains, and the world is fed:

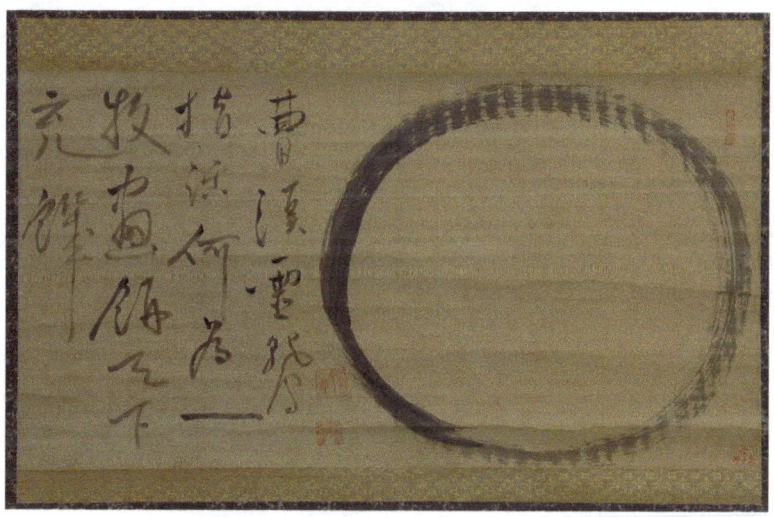

Anonymous calligraphy, 1850, ink on paper.

The text and the drawing enhance the deep meaning of the circle in Japanese culture, where the simple act of drawing produces an artwork with many other layers and a deep and nurturing meaning: the world is full.

Another title and calligraphy of the artist Ubeko Kosan (1695–1633) empathizes the other different aspects of the circle. *On the rock there is a jar. In there is a cosmos. Nobody holds the truth, I muse on void.*

Ubako Kosen, 17th century calligraphy, Ink on paper

The circle represents both the complexity of the infinity and the emptiness that lies in our existence. It combines the essence of the void, the vacuum, with the essence of the extent—the being. We can also learn about the fierceness and the simplicity that exist simultaneously in the circle from a habit that takes place in certain places in Japanese culture, according to which, once a circle is drawn, it should not be touched. That way, it will remain as a testimony to the figure of the person who drew it, and to his abilities, which were expressed in the blink of an eye by the drawing of a simple, round line.

Paul Klee, "Ad Marignem," 1930, Basel Art Museum

We can look at the circle as a theme which also has great importance in contemporary art, using the very same symbolism of the simple and the complex, the memories and the repetition.

This painting, by the Swiss artist Paul Klee (1879-1940), one of the 20th century's most influential artists, demonstrates, along with many other paintings and scraps taken from his diary, how children's drawings and geometric shapes, (and the circle among them), have been an inspiration for his compositions. This became a foundation for his explorations—and an aid in trying to understand the order within the chaos.

Here is another example of the use that was made of the circle in a contemporary art work by Yael Balaban:

Target Game of Dreams 45x45cm, touches and pyrography on mazonite, 2010.

Dressed Man 112x75 cm, ink on paper (after J.E. Marey), 2014.

These circular designs that started as doodles all carry different meanings with them: memories, a discovery of one's identity, revival and creation. The inspiration for these art works was born out of the artist's own personal story; a cursive signature that was discovered among family manuscripts inspired her, was imprinted in her memory and eventually became a source for her work.

Another example is taken from the multi-disciplinary artist Ram Samocha, an artist who mixes drawings with various other media of art such as photography, performance, animation and video. In this work, he shares the process of marking the birth of a circle with his viewers:

Ram Samocha—
An installation of drawing with silicone; photography: Marco Baradi.
This was created at the international symposium of drawing and
performance "Draw to Perform" in London, 2015. This image is a detail taken from six hours of drawing on paper two meters in diameter.

Ram Samocha—
An installation of drawing with colorful pencils, 2009, photographed
documentation in a studio, Ontario, Canada.

The shape of the circle is not as simple as it seems. It is a symbolic shape containing within it an entire universe. All these meanings and strengths, as well as the unique place the circle holds in different cultures and in the art world, can also be experienced by you, once the circle is born in your own toddler's drawings, in the most intuitive and natural way, when he creates a shape and a world of his own—all out of the "scribble" and the doodle.

The circle:
a separate shape, representing the birth of a "me," in light of its surroundings.

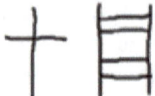

C | The cross has come and, with it, complexity:
ages three to four

After the circle appears, the shape of a cross—or the shape of a ladder—will form out of the doodles and lines. This is the encounter between vertical and horizontal lines. When the child draws a cross, a graphic expression is obtained, representing a significant emotional development: the beginning of reciprocal relations.

Take a few minutes to observe the cross. What do you see? Two opposing lines that cross one another and meet in the middle. It is very simple, yet also very complex. The cross represents one's acceptance of oppositions such as up and down, horizontal and vertical, left and right and Earth and sky, as well as more abstract oppositions such as spirit and matter, fantasy and reality.

Drawing the cross represents the acquisition of a new orientation in space, the transition from crawling (horizontal and leaning) to standing (vertical and independent) and the relationship and connection between the lines that were formed. It is a viewpoint out of which one is able to walk forwards, backwards, and to the sides.

The horizontal axis is the spatial axis, an axis which represents the connection with the outer world, the ability to give to others as well as to receive. It can also represent the ground and earthliness, or the daily routine. The vertical axis, on the other hand, which is centered, represents independence, and being able to "stand on one's feet." At the lower end, this axis expresses a sense of corporeality, anchoring, stability and intensity, and when it rises up it represents common sense, thinking, imagination and spirituality.

Both axes need each other and are dependent on one another; they are inseparable in the development process of the child and man.

The cross can also represent the experience of an intersection—an intersection of spaces, a crossroads, and various possibilities, along with determination and finding the path. Between the poles, the middle point appears—a point of connection and meeting. Meeting points are much like insights gathered from different sources, which intersect and continue on their path toward new creative grounds. The meeting between the two lines creates a point and an internal axis (centeredness).

We can see that the meeting point connects the two lines and holds them together. This creates a sense of three dimensions, invisible but still perceived, and it is very significant. It expresses the feeling that there's something inside, that there's a depth to it. This experiential interior serves as a symbolic vessel where one can store thoughts, memories and imaginings, and also emotional occurrences that are present, despite being invisible.

The psychoanalyst Frances Tustin writes:

"I can only say that the stage at which they make a vertical straight line and a horizontal straight line of the same length to intersect in a right-angled way has always proved to be a significant stage in psychotherapy.

"Also, when this occurs, the children develop the sense of being able to hold good things inside their body. Until this stage is reached, they have no notion of insides, but relate only to surfaces. For example, the hard back is not connected to the soft front by the inside of the body.

Front and back are two separate, discrete surfaces, and hardness and softness are opposites which seem incompatible with each other.

As the qualities of hardness and softness become connected with each other, more subtle combinations come into awareness. Also, as there develops the notion of insides which cannot be seen, touched or handled but which can link and hold things together, there develops the sense of having a 'mind' associated with such unseen mental events as thoughts, fantasies and memories. The processes by which this occurs in therapy seem bizarre to our sophisticated minds used to dealing with abstractions, but something like the following occurs."

Yes, this is a little complicated, indeed. The innocent cross that the child has drawn is allegedly only a meeting point between vertical and horizontal lines, but, in reality, it is much more complicated and meaningful. It teaches us about the child's inner emotional world which has become a lot more complex, and it can now bear the concept of oppositions and allow the imagination and independent thoughts to form and to grow.

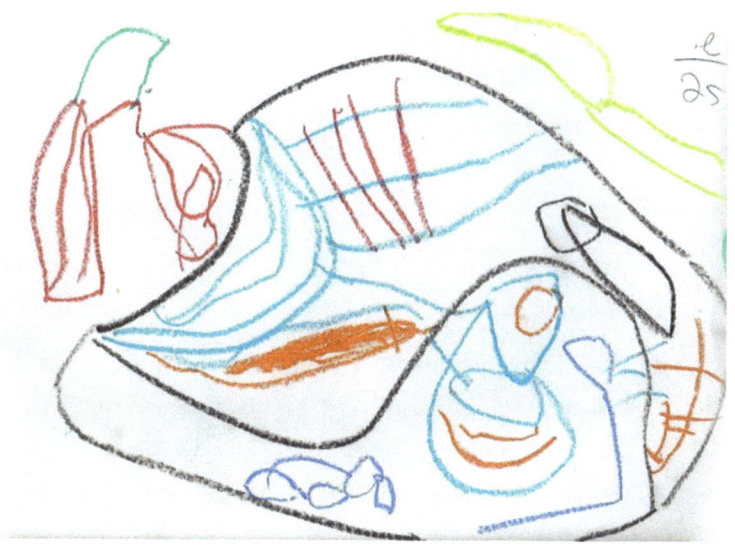

Examples of crosses and ladders:

More examples of crosses and ladders:

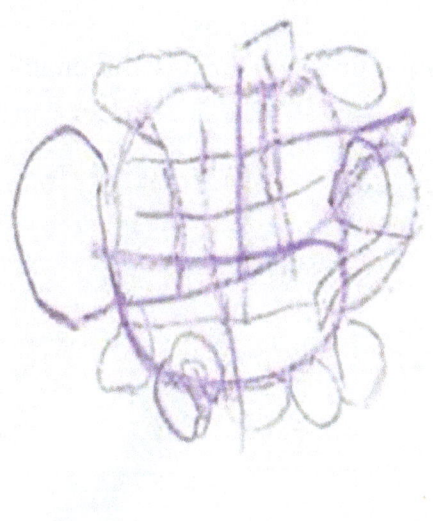

The cross:
a shape that contains oppositions and enables balance
and an acceptance of one's inner world.

D | This dot is me:
ages three to four

The parallel stage to creating a cross is that of creating a dot—a dot which will be created, this time inside the circle, and will dwell inside it. It's nice to dwell inside the circle and to be granted "custody." This brings a sense of security and acceptance. The circle does not have any cracks or corners, and it is sealed from every direction.

A dot (or a cross) created inside the circle will represent the "me," the center of the self, that "something" which is good within me, the essence of liveliness, the vitality that is being held and protected in its shell. They can also represent the feelings and thoughts that come into being and grow inside of it. The knowledge that feelings and thoughts exist also outside of "me" then begins to form and develop.

What is inside of me is me, what is outside of me isn't me, Winnicott claims. The ability to think "within me" about things that exist "outside of me" represents the development of the imagination.

A dot drawn inside while intending, pausing, withholding, delaying and gathering, resembles the process of accumulating energy and preparing for facing outwards. So yes, the dot can teach us a lot about the child's emotional growth.

Examples of dots formed inside the circle:

More crosses and dots:

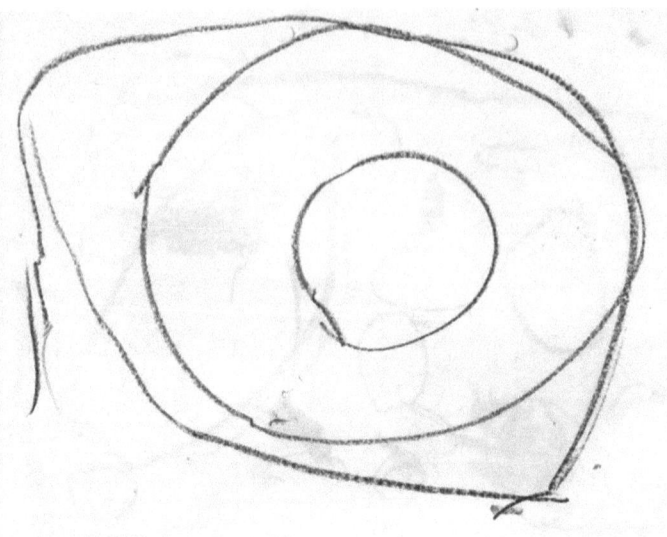

The dot (or cross) inside the circle:
something is alive inside of me.

E | The circle has grown horns: ages three to four

After the drawing of the circle, lines that are attached to the circle begin to appear growing out of it like horns. These horns, reaching out from the circle, will begin to form—and not coincidently. It will happen right after the dot in the middle appears. Only then, **out of the confidence that there is a "me" inside, one can reach outside toward the "other."**

This development of the lines, spreading outwards, expresses the uniqueness of the "me" of the drawing infant, and the ability to have a dialogue, to communicate, to give and to love the other.

Something inside of him is now willing and capable of going outside toward a new path.

Circles that have horns growing out of them.

More horns that grew out of the circles.

Horns:
The way to the outside world and to a connection
with the "other."

F | A base has appeared, here comes the triangle: ages four to five and up

In the next stage, the child draws a triangle. Unlike the circle, which is created out of one infinite, flowing and cursive line, the triangle is created out of three straight lines that come together with sharp angles, in a movement that requires a sudden turn. The ability to create a triangle with three separate lines that form into shape at one point, is an ability that requires planning, emotional development and higher motor and cognitive abilities than those that the circle or the doodle require.

Mario Livio, the astronomer and a scientist, has worked in the fields of art and mathematics, and states in his book The Golden Ratio how, in the Sumerian language of Mesopotamia, it was implied that every number bigger than two is considered to be a lot. (The digit three was mentioned as an "ace" and was interpreted as a multiplicity.)

The same logic works for the child. Drawing a shape made of three lines is a lot more than drawing with one or two lines. This resembles, perhaps, the transition from being a couple to becoming a family of three: creating the three edges of the triangle may, therefore, suggest that the child is now aware of more complex relationships. Triangular relationships, such as, for instance mother-father-child, or child-brother-sister, kindergarten teacher-child-and-another-child; these are relationships that require a much greater emotional ability than dual relationships.

At this age, according to Sigmund Freud, begins the "Oedipus Complex", that relates to triangle relationship in which the child feels competition and envy toward the parent of his own sex, derived by his wish and desire to become the partner of the other parent's spouse. We can see that playing father-mother- child is very typical in much of the role playing that takes place in children around that age.

One line of the triangle is the base line, a line that represents stability and confidence, and expresses the continuing internalization of the construction of an inner self within the child, and the perception that he is now a part of a triangle – a family.

Drawing a triangle with sharp angles can also express dynamism, assertiveness and a sense of direction like that of an arrow.

Triangles offer many possibilities and directions. We can see in the examples various shapes of the triangle, and among them different empathies, sometimes in shapes that were drawn by the same child—the tip of the triangle, the stable basis, the open basis. Each child shows his own style, personality, pace, and different rhythms within him.

The triangle, much like the cross and the circle, holds great meaning and importance in different cultures. Some connect it with spirituality, such as the Star of David in Judaism, or the Holy Trinity in Christianity. In Buddhism, it's used as an aid for meditation, and in Islam the star represents Godliness and sovereignty.

It's as though spiritual symbolism springs out of the triangle's dynamism, and also out of the movement between the upper and lower world of the edges of the triangle's tip.

The tip of the triangle facing upwards represents facing beyond earthliness, routine and vagueness. It represents the skies, the crown, wisdom, understanding and consciousness.

The triangle with its tip facing down represent the lower world of earthliness and the senses.

The poet Leah Goldberg writes in her poem: On three things the world stands

The fisherman said;
On three things the world stands The sea's water
The land's shores
And the deep sea's fish caught up by the net

The poem goes on, and each time, from a different point of view, the world stands on three different things.

Many of our basic concepts and perceptions of the world are derived out of the number three—the number of the triangle's edges.

The child, in a very admirable manner, and in a natural and intuitive way, draws and produces basic shapes that conceal the meanings unique to him, and revealing his development in parallel to the many different meanings that have been given to the very same shapes in different cultures throughout history.

Examples of triangles.

Triangle:
grounds for confidence, dynamism and relationships that are expanding.

Chapter Five

Can I now bring a figure to life?:

ages four to six

Once the child has the motor abilities needed to create a circle, a dot, vertical and horizontal lines, sharp ones as well as cursive ones, and the ability to join them together, he is able to construct and assemble a figure.

In drawing a figure, it's as though the child is creating a person and an entire world. Drawing now has so much power! The child, as Erno Stern says is the undisputed owner of the world he created.

He is its center, its engine and its commander. In most cases, the figure will be one of the first representative objects drawn by the child, because of the interest in the "self" and the significance and the meaning of the people in his world.

The first drawings of a figure are created out of a subjective experience of body perception that is typical of children at these ages, which is why the figures will not appear as imitations of the body in real life.

In the beginning, the figure will be marked as a symbol, in a more general way with no uniqueness or gender. A relative sent me a video of her three-year-old daughter, who had drawn three identical circles. The child explained that the first circle was a girl, the second one, she explained (in a soft and sweet voice) was a boy, and the third circle she presented (in a serious and assertive voice) as a policeman. Every time I look at this video I smile because of the graceful manner in which the child has presented the three identical circles as three completely different characters.

The process of drawing a figure, as we've seen with this child, will start with the drawing of the circle, which is the most familiar and approachable shape for the child. In it the child will mark a head. The head will be drawn big, probably out of the child's understanding and sense that the head is a very important organ: it is where the mouth, nose and eyes are, all of which have very important roles (seeing, eating, speaking, smelling and breathing) and they serve as the organs that communicate with the outside world.

At this stage, the body and the head in the painting will not be separated. This lack of separation, perhaps, expresses graphically the emotional and bodily "lumpy" ex-perience that is typical at this stage of inseparability.

Later on, out of the "body-head," hand and leg shaped lines will appear, in a stage which is called the "tadpole."

That way, when the child's consciousness of himself as a separate object evolves—as seen by the outside world—his figure drawings will be influenced accordingly, and will increasingly come to resemble a real human being; this is, of course, accompanied by the development of his motor abilities.

The head serves also as a body, from which hand and leg shaped lines come out.

Interestingly, the order and the process in which the child draws the figure resembles the order of development of the first shapes drawn by him. Usually, the order is as follows: first, the face (a circle), later on, the child will draw the eyes (like the dot inside the circle), after that, he will draw the legs, which express the ability to stand on one's feet (like the vertical lines), and then he will draw the hands, which represent the connection with the outside world (much like the horns that came out of the circle after the dot inside it was drawn). Eventually the feet will appear (the base line of the triangle, the grounding).

One may look at the drawing of the figure with the hands and legs as similar to the shape of the cross; they express the balance and complexity that are characteristic of the cross.

The crosses and the figure combine.

Around the age of four or five, the emotional process of separateness continues to influence the way the figure is drawn. At this age, the child may draw a separate circle for the head, and another circle (or other shapes) to mark the body. The legs will now come out of the center of the body and not out of the head, in a way that closely resembles a real human body.

In more advanced stages, around the age of six, the process of separateness, as well as the child's graphic abilities, continue to evolve and become more sophisticated. Often, the head and the body will be separated by a neck, and the fingers will be separated from one another and from the hand. All of these make the bodily experience a lot less "lumpy."

Later on, the child's ability to symbolize and imagine will expand. Slowly, organs will receive more volume and will become more three-dimensional. This will create the feeling that there is something in there. The individual expressions in the figure drawings evolve and become more sophisticated. From approximately ages six to nine, the movements and positions, the differences in size and other precise details (such as the hair, the teeth, fingers, eyebrows and more) will begin to appear and, with them, also the figure's gender and its uniqueness. All these express an identity that has now evolved, as well as the acknowledgement of the existence of an "other" that is different.

The body and the head are separate. More specific characteristics: the boy differs from the girl.

Later on, more objects or people will join the figure that, up until now, has appeared mostly on its own. This will create a much more complex environment. When my son, a computer buff, was in kindergarten and was asked to draw his family, he added a computer "standing" near his father, mother and sister. Relationships begin to form between the different figures and objects, and more complex compositions now take place. At this stage, the child already has awareness of space, he knows how to divide the page into "up" and "down," and his figures are standing on the ground underneath the skies. Up until this point, the figure that was the center of the world, is now no longer the biggest and most central figure.

There is no longer only one central figure, as more figures join.

Despite having the same order of development in the figure drawings, the pace of development may differ from child to child, and many times one may see gaps, even in drawings created by the same child. A hand picking a flower in a child's drawing can be longer than the figure that stands doing nothing.

In the following examples, we can see how some drawings have figures with legs coming out of their heads and others with legs coming out of the center of their body (a more realistic perception).

The differences between the drawings are influenced by varying motor ability, emotional experiences, and the amount of importance given by the child to the different figures and organs.

Drawings with different figures that reflect the gaps in the stages of development: in one, the legs are coming out of the head, while another shows them coming out of the body center.

Legs coming out of the body | Legs coming out of the head

Another example of legs coming out of the body or out of the head.

Legs coming out of the body | Legs coming out of the head

And to anyone who asks when trees, flowers and animal start appearing—they will arrive, and perhaps have already arrived, sometime after the "tadpoles" (the body-head stage) in the first stages of the figure drawings. Once the line and circle join, they will become either flowers or trees, and if you play a little bit and turn the figure horizontally and add a short or long tail, "real" animals of all kinds and sorts will start forming.

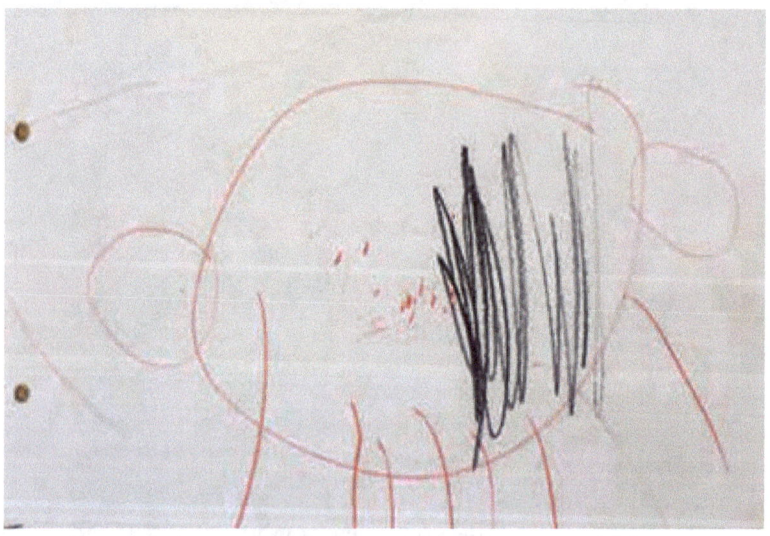

Circles placed horizontally create all sorts of animals.

A line and a circle have turned into flowers and trees.

Chapter Six

How to build a house— or a house isn't only a square:
ages four to five

By the time the child has discovered how to create lines for a base, a triangle and a square, his imagination has evolved and his understanding of the real world has extended. An ability to plan and join the different elements now exists within him—and a house can be "built"!

The house's lower part is the square, a shape that consists of four lines. This is a shape that holds meanings of stability, structure, and grounding within it, and can represent materialism and an understanding of reality.

On top of that, one cannot ignore the fact that the house in its essence is also symbolic and holds emotional meanings. The concept of the house, for the child, relates to the experience of a family. Inside his house, his family resides. Therefore, the house will represent protection and shelter, a cover, a safe place to settle, and, on a certain level, a place where he can be protected by adults who take care of him.

Normally, the child will draw the frame of the square first, and above it he will usually draw the roof as a triangle. This triangle resembles, perhaps, the head placed above the body, or a cover offering protection to the residents of the house, and possibly represents, the spiritual being above the material. We can also look at the triangle in a drawing of a house as a shape that represents the three different "edges" of the family: mother, father and child.

Usually, around the age of six, windows and a door are added to these drawings, perhaps resembling eyes and a mouth—and they create a division between the exterior and the interior. The windows are like openings in the house, through which one can look. This experience of looking is two-sided: one can observe from the inside outwards (to the "other") and also from the outside in (the "other" observing you). The same thing goes for the door: through it, one can exit, leaving the private world of the interior, and entering the outer world that belongs to the "others," and vice versa. These openings are a metaphor for the child's emotional processes and can represent accessibility to others.

Drawings of a house with windows and a door are created at a pace along with significant characteristics that differ from child to child. A child can empathize or withhold from a certain element of the house according to the meaning and importance it had for him while he was drawing and exploring the world and himself.

Different types of houses.

Drawing a house—a base and a ground. One may enter it or leave it.

Chapter Seven

All the colors of emotions—drawing with color

"Color, such a deep language and mysterious, the language of dreams."
Paul Gauguin

When I sat down to write this chapter on the development of color schemes in children, I came across emotional blockages. I was worried that a cognitive distance and an analytic exploration of color and the process of its development might spoil some of the color's magic.

The Dutch painter, Piet Mondrian, wrote: "The color alone has the ability to revive everything, and a pure observation of color can be extremely spiritual."

Having overcome my worries, I discovered that the development of a color scheme also has a fixed order, and that this order is, of course, influenced by the child's cognitive and emotional development. The order of color use resembles the process of progression from doodling to drawing figures, although the transitions between the different stages are far less evident.

Usually, children add colors to their drawings before the age of three, during the process of developing lines and shapes. At this stage, the experience of drawing is primarily a physical and sensory one, much like with the doodle. The child draws and paints as a part of a game, while he explores the world around him. Much like at the doodling stage, the joy the result brings him motivation to want to continue, to experiment and explore the different colors in a sensory, motorial, and playful manner.

At this stage, the child does not recognize the colors by their names, and he chooses them according to his emotion and intuition. Later on, around the age of three, as his experimentation with the use of different colors progresses, there is a transition from a linear style of coloring (such as the doodle) to coloring specks and surfaces. The manner in which specks are spread, and how numerous they are, expresses a change in the child's experience with a transition into a more carefree and flowing movement, one which reflects the expansion of his emotional world.

A linear type of coloring.

Spreading an unrecognized color.

The colors are now separate.

The development of a color scheme continues to mature along with motor and cognitive skills, and as the child's perception of self as a separate "me" comes into being. Moving from a world of chaos, of spreading and meddling with unrecognized and undistinguished color, into a world of distinction, preference and choice, he now expresses individuality: the child, from ages three to five, is usually able to distinguish between the different colors and to name them. Despite his ability to distinguish between the different colors, his color choice is still intuitive and he doesn't go by the color of the object he's painting, but rather by his emotions and subjective feelings: the figure might be painted red because, "Today is my birthday," and the sun blue because, "Mommy and Daddy went away," and so on.

Later on, around ages five to seven, the child's color choice comes much closer to reality. In other words, the connection between the object's real colors to the colors chosen by the child becomes tighter. The sun will now be painted yellow, the grass green and so on. The child's perception comes much closer to reality, as we saw with the course of development of shapes.

At that stage, the child's experimentation with color mixing will continue to expand and to enrich. The child experiments with different mixes and combinations, and is often surprised by the change in colors and the variety of shades that form during this process. The ability to reach many shades and colors reflects his ability to express and to bear a much wider and richer scale of emotions. Through the many shades and possibilities created with his use of color, the child learns that an infinity of paths is now open to him. Color becomes a tool that enables the child to have more flexibility and deepen his emotional world.

Multiple colors allow him to experiment and reflect the emotional experience that is forming in his world in a more accurate way, much like the way a wider vocabulary enables him to narrate himself better to his environment.

"This color is too red, and now with the white I've added, the color is light and lifeless. Now I add yellow and I get a peachy color, which is just right for me."

This is a quote of a patient during her process of finding the right color to express her emotions. It is a unique moment, one in which, after searching, the child (or the adult) finds the color or shade that accurately echoes his own feeling, leading to an experience that is authentic, soothing and empowering. It's as though something inside him is now clearer, as if his "me" becomes clearer and more accurate.

New shades have come into being.

The beginning of planning and choice, and the separateness of color.

In time, a reciprocal relationship between the different colors in the drawing is formed, one that may reflect the development of a relationship between the child and the "other," and with his environment.

One girl remarked while looking at her drawing: "How come the same color looks different when I place it next to the red and when I place it next to the blue."

A boy created a competition between the different colors: "Let's see which one's stronger, the black or the purple."

Another patient came to a therapy session in an emotional storm. She started painting with gouache paints—at the beginning, red and yellow doodles at the center of the paper, and at some point she started to produce very organized blue circles around the doodles. In our mutual observation in the aftermath of drawing, that girl realized that she'd expressed her emotional upset in the yellow and red doodles, colors which she perceived as "stormy." Later on, in order to soothe herself, or perhaps in order to appear more balanced outside, she'd painted blue circles ("a color and a shape which are quiet and soothing") around the red and yellow doodles. She summarized the process excitedly: "Now I can see that the order of the colors is not coincidental."

This is how Henri Matisse described the reciprocal relationship between the painter and his colors:

"I laid the first color of the painting, added a second color, and then, instead
of dismissing it when it seemed unsuitable to the first color,
I laid a third color with the intention of creating an affinity between them.
Then, I had to continue in the same manner, until I sensed I had created the
perfect harmony in my painting, and that I have unloaded the feeling which
made me paint it in the first place."

In this manner, through the choice of color, (warm or cold, light or dark, conspicuous or hidden, opposite or alike) and through the order in which the colors appear and are placed on the page (close and touching each other, or distant and separated) the child is given another way of experimenting and learning about the reciprocal relationship between the diverse emotions of his inner world and the people outside, who shape and construct his perception of self as a part of the system in which he exists.

Different colors hold different meanings that influence and stimulate emotional reactions. the warm yellow will have a different influence than cold blue.

Kandinsky writes:
"On the whole, keen colours are well suited by sharp forms (e.g. a yellow
triangle), and soft, deep colours by round forms (e.g., a blue circle),"

The different meanings are influenced by physiological and cultural factors, and by changing subjective emotions. White color on white paper can express a feeling of invisibility or death, as well as serenity and a new beginning. Black can express sadness, anxiety, death, or drama, intensity and respect. Red can express love or hurt, life or death. A thirty-year-old patient used to draw a white circle around her drawings, which expressed—in her words—the death of her father, which stopped her vitality from expressing itself since. In later stages of the therapy she colored the stomach of colorful fish white, which she associated with pregnancy and coming back to life, lots of joy and vitality. In one drawing, the color symbolized death, and in the other it symbolized a new life and a new beginning.

The approach toward color differs from person to person (child or adult) and changes according to the unique situation and association of the painter and of the observer. This is why it is important and interesting to pay attention to the different meanings and possibilities, to respect them and to be open and attentive to them.

Here are a few examples of color being used to express emotion in children's drawings.

An angry child and a reconciling child: colors have changed.

This is a drawing, divided into two, by a ten-year-old who hit a child in his class. It's a depiction of the reconciliation between the two children. One can see the difference in colors. The legs in the upper painting are painted red, expressing anger, while the legs in the lower painting, on the other hand, are brown – a color that expresses grounding and relaxation. On top of that, both the movement and the eyes, which were added to the drawing, express a connection and emphasize the message of transferring from anger to calmness.

The house of an eight-year-old just starting therapy, and during therapy (six months later).

These are paintings by an eight-year-old who came to therapy when he was very sad and withdrawn. In the beginning he chose to paint with very few dark colors (the upper painting). During the process of therapy, a few months later, he chose colors that were a lot lighter and much more diverse (the lower painting). This indicates that the child is much calmer, open and happy.

Use of color is a wonderful way of expressing different emotions such as anger, sadness, vitality, flow, freedom and joy. Color may disturb, intimidate, awaken, soothe, heal, bind or charm. Experimenting with color is a very meaningful tool for deepening the emotional world.

Colors—an expression of the emotional world.

Chapter Eight

A private collection from doodling to drawing a figure
—by a girl and a boy

If you look at the albums and binders where your own children's photos are kept, you could, possibly, assemble a sequence showing a process of transformation, from doodling to drawing a figure; it is the fruit of your child's labors. The following drawings were given to me from the private collections of mothers. It's fascinating.

The development sequence of the girl's drawings:

Doodle.

The circle that was created out of the doodle.

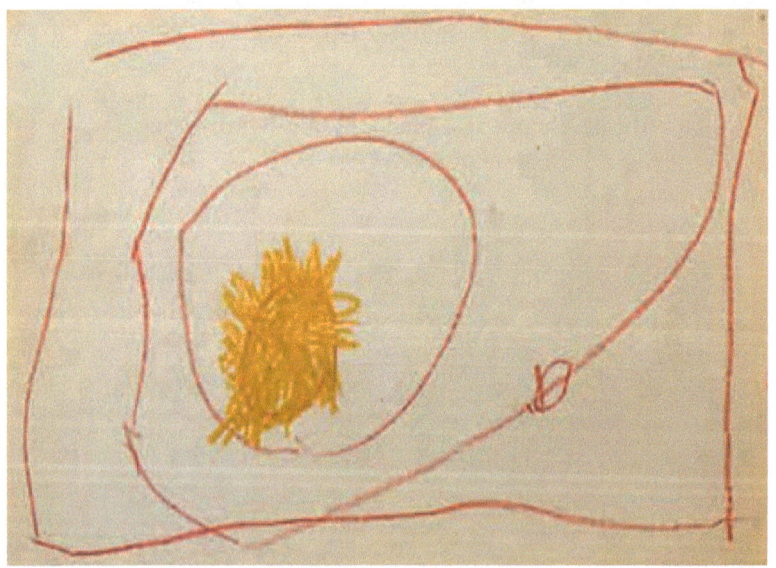

A dot inside the circle.

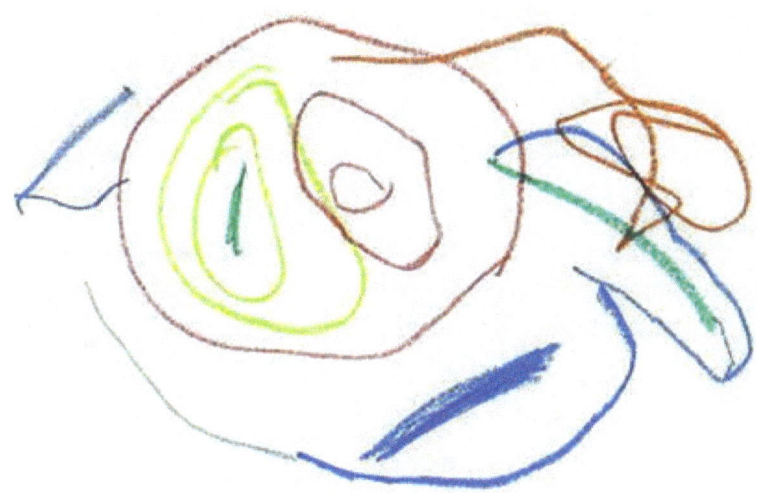

Another dot inside the circle.

Crosses.

A "tadpole."

Figures with characterization and an environment.

The development sequence of the boy's drawings:

Doodling.

Circles.

The dot inside the circle, horns come out, and the cross is formed.

Primary figures and their environment.

A figure with characterization and its environment.

Chapter Nine

From the doodle to the circle— a universal phenomenon

One interesting thing about doodling and the development of children's drawings is the universal grounding of this process. Children from different cultures normally draw in a similar manner. Rhoda Kellogg (1898-1987), who was among the first researchers and collectors of children's drawings, collected around half a million children's drawings from thirty different countries, and published her research in her book Analyzing Children's Art.

Out of the many drawings she collected throughout the years, Kellogg concluded that there is a manner of expression that is similar in all cultures—a broad, universal common process of development in all stages of children's drawings, and that the same common denominator is mainly related to the sequence of the mental, emotional and physiological development—not necessarily to the influence of the environment.

Kellogg believed that the drawings are archetypical, naturally imprinted. Prof Ben Ami Scharfstein, in his book Birds, Elephants and Other Artists, has stated that young children all around the world will apparently, once given the chance, develop in a similar manner: first they will doodle, then they will move to simple shapes and compositions, and eventually to more complex ones. According to Prof Scharfstein, graphic interpretations all over the world will always be common and also resemble one another.

Arno Stern, the pioneer of creative education, who worked with children as of the Second World War, concluded from his experiments and from his great experiences around the world, that creation springs out of an organic force, a need which is imprinted in man. From 1967 to1972, Stern travelled around the world and examined drawings of children who were not influenced by school and whose lifestyle was characterized by their environment. He searched for wanderers; he lived in small villages in Africa, lived with rain forest people in the Amazon and in the jungles of New Guinea. Out of the many drawings he saw and collected, he found that there is a formal developmental structure—"formalization" as he called it—to the graphic language, and it is universal.

Stern describes how he gave a sheet of paper to a rainforest child and a desert child and the children spontaneously filled it with shapes and forms. Stern continues to describe how, with each passing day, the sheets were filled with round shapes, horns, cloaks and all possible shapes. They drew on dozens of sheets in a row, diverse, and continuing. According to him, none of the children had ever seen a pencil, a pen or crayons, yet they all knew immediately what to do with them, and used them without hesitation as though it was an essential human act.

In preparation for writing this book, I asked everyone I know who traveled or worked abroad, to bring me children's drawings from different countries, and I invited people from all around the world on the internet, on parents forums and on Facebook, to send me drawings done by their children for this book. It is interesting to see that, despite the technological development, early efforts at drawing do not change. The drawing starts out at the same point: doodles, lines and circles, later evolving into figures. This is true, and it applies anywhere around the world.

Samples of doodles from Germany:
boy approximately two-and-a-half/three years old.

The beginning of circle drawing, another boy from Germany.

United States, aged nine months.

A drawing from China by a one-and-a-half-year-old boy.

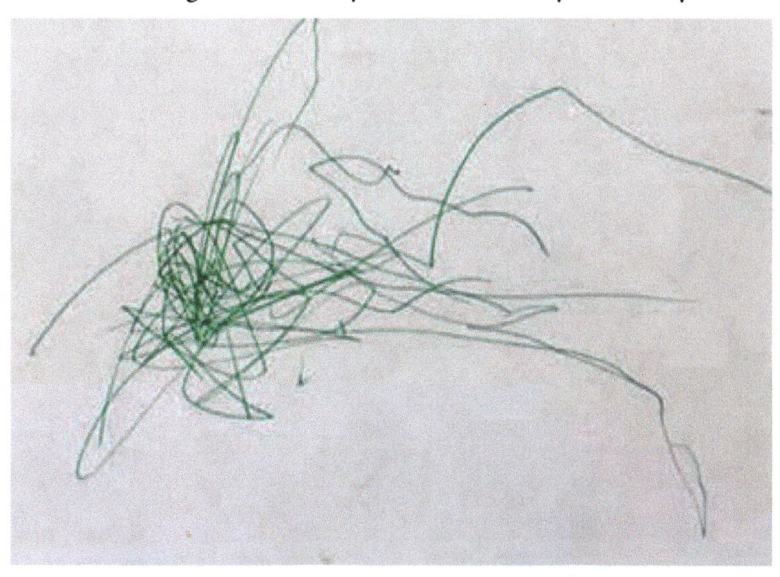

A drawing by a four-year-old girl from Sweden.

Drawings by children around two years old from Eritrea.

More drawings from Eritrea.

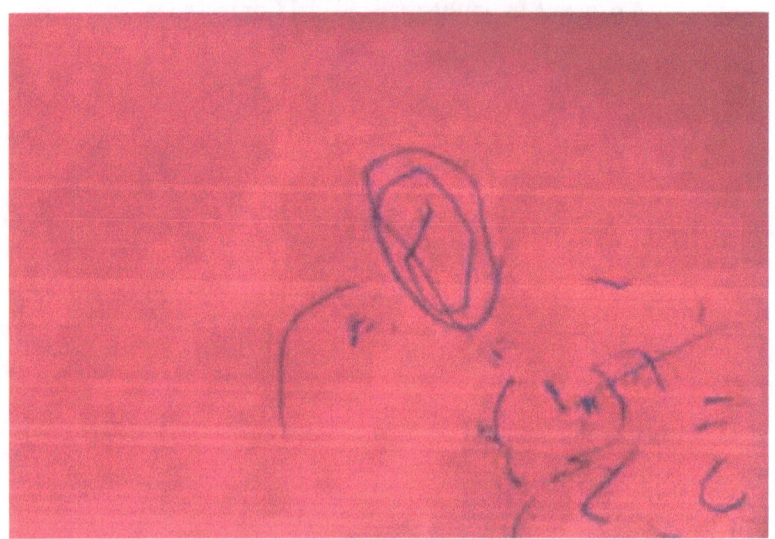

Drawings by kindergarten children from Singapore, aged five to six.

More drawings from Singapore.

Drawings from Africa—a four-year-old boy.

Drawing a figure—a four-year-old boy from Ireland.

A drawing from Switzerland, by a five-year-old boy.

Drawing from France, by a five-year-old boy.

Chapter Ten

The soul, the doodle, and circles in adults

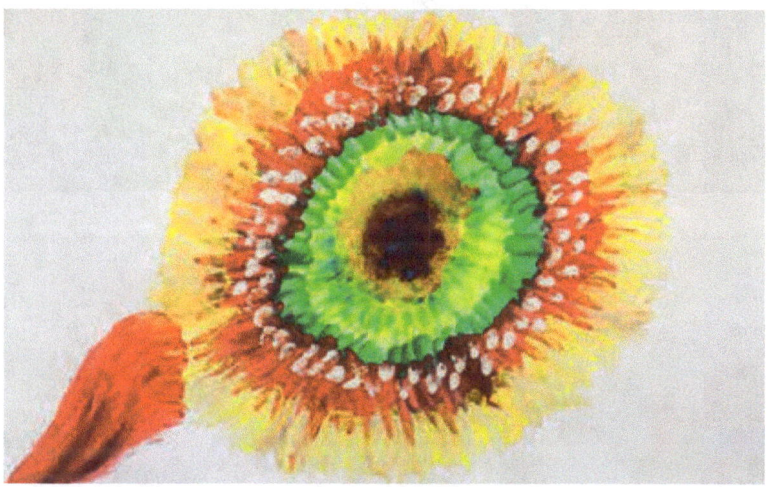

Examples of circles in adult drawings that were formed spontaneously during therapy.

It's interesting to see how the development sequence of children's drawings, which I have described in the previous chapters, returns and appears in adult drawings. All the stages from the different ages are present in adult drawings, with the doodle, the circle, the dot inside the circle, the cross and the triangle, often representing the same meanings: playfulness, strong emotions, confusion, separateness, breaking outside, and finding the "me."

Normally adults come with more awareness, depth and complexity, but nonetheless, there is sometimes a need to come back to the primary stages of the drawing, whether it is due to the patient being inexperienced, or whether out of a need to correct them, or simply out of missing the good that one has experienced during his childhood.

Sometimes, a natural cycle of coming back to the primal world simply occurs, and out of it one can grow and flourish, in drawing and in life in general.

In some of the cases, I was assisted by the "focusing" method, in order to deepen and aid the processes that occur, and to allow the insight to emerge.

The "focusing" method was founded in the seventies by Eugene T. Gendlin, a philosopher and psychologist. The focusing method is an open method that can be combined with other therapeutic methods. It's based on a process of listening to the private inner experience, and attending to the feelings of the body and to the sensual and visual images which arise. In this method, one listens to the answer that comes from deep within him, without any judgement or criticism for whatever comes up, from ambiguous feelings to more focused and clear emotions, that might clarify and focus thoughts and contemplations.

The combination of the focusing method with psychotherapy and art therapy is another tool for expressing the feelings that emerge out of our inner world with more clarity and accuracy.

This chapter shows samples from processes that occur with adult drawings: doodles, circles, triangles and crosses.

A doodle by a fifty-year-old woman, demonstrating the expression of her emotional state during a confusing situation.

A | The circle within

The attainable   **The desirable.**

The body image as a free image.

These two drawings were drawn by Ruti, a thirty-five-year-old woman who was preoccupied with the question of body image. I asked her to draw her body image as it is today, and also her desired body image. At first (the drawing on top) she drew two body images. The figure on the left represents the body image as it is today—the attainable, with circles scattered outside the body—and the one on the right represents her desirable body image. Right after, she added a spontaneous body image, this time of a container with circles inside (the bottom drawing) as a representative of the desirable body image and she said, "This is it. This feels like a much more authentic and accurate expression of the body I'd like to have." Perhaps, in this manner of expression, Ruti felt as though the container and circles that were now inside represented her "self" as a more authentic and whole being, more accepting and more protected.

Later on, when I asked Ruti's permission to use the drawings for my book, I received this poem as an addition to the drawings:

I lay circles out of myself Emit unwanted knots Like a cat
I ruminate Feelings
There are results A more fit body with Remnants of what
Has been On paper
In art and in therapy There is evidence Circle

Throughout the years, I have seen many circles being formed spontaneously during therapy sessions. Sometimes, the circle expressed strength and consolidation, a safe haven, while other times it expressed one being withdrawn and the desire to be more open and outgoing. Sometimes, the circle is experienced as soft and pleasant, while at other times an intimidating experience of weakness lies beneath this softness.

Sometimes the circle felt empty and airy for the patient, while, at certain times, this emptiness expressed pain. Sometimes the circle, full of color, was experienced by the patient as too compressed, while at other times it was full and nurturing.

A circle that was experienced as compressed. The white color was added intuitively to air this compression.

A patient who made a clay circle described it rolling and moving around and added: "Sometimes we're up and sometimes we're down. It's a cycle."

Another patient wanted me to draw a pink circle for her on the paper, as a safe haven inside in which she could place and draw her own personal content.

B | From doodling to drawing a circle with horns

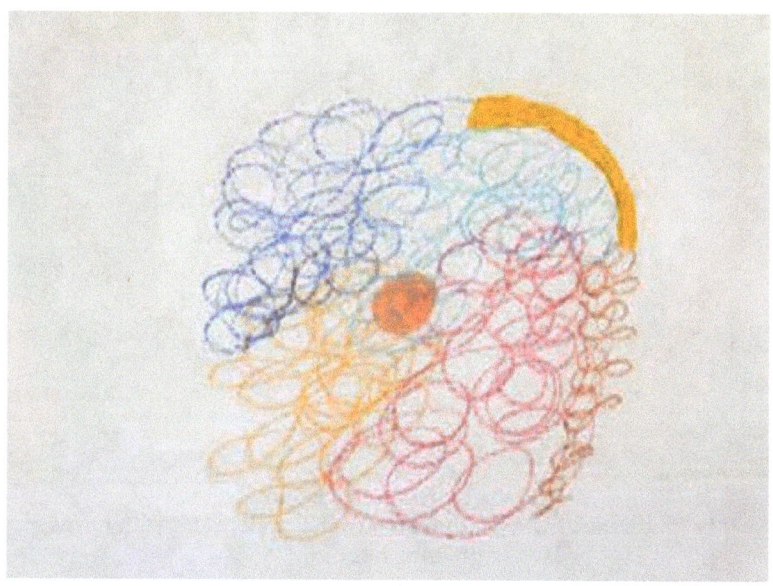

Noa's drawing.
The circle, representing the "me," is revealed by the doodle's
entanglement. "The pink is like the body and it is attached."

Noa, thirty years old, came to therapy in order to strengthen her self-es-teem and to find out what could help her in creating a healthy, committed relationship. During therapy sessions, Noa created doodles out of which she discovered her circle—the "me," in pink. Every time she noticed its presence, it made her feel happy. It was as if, each time she experienced her "me" once again, she felt its existence safe within her. When she observed the circle painted pink, she said, "This is me," or, "The pink is like a body attached." Along the process, she drew lines coming out of the circle, much like horns, and she remarked: "This is my breakthrough." She named the drawing, "An Explosion of a Hug."

How is all of this connected to the subject that brought her to therapy?

Using the shapes created and the meaning that was given to them, Noa, with time, went through a process of constructing a separate and inde-pendent identity. This was a process of integration between childhood and adulthood. When she described the colors she chose for the circles, she said that the pink represented her childish softness, orange represented the feminine, green the mature and assertive—and they all lay within her.

The storm that created a flower:
My "outbreak" from the doodle into the circle, a dot with horns growing out of it.

The more mature "me," made out of various colors.

The drawings also echoed her feelings—the outbreak and emotional storm she experienced, and the anger toward her parents that emerged during therapy. This process helped her to construct and form her separate independence (represented by the pink circle) and later on enabled her to come to terms with the house in which she grew up, to acknowledge her own roots, and learn how to love and accept them more. The reconciliation, the liberation of the anger and the acceptance of the more meaningful figures in her life, along with the experience of an authentic "self," paved the way for her toward forming a relationship.

In this manner, the whole meaningful process started with the doodle and finding the circle which emerged out of it.

C | The circle and the meaning of life

The meaning of life is being me.

The drawing above was drawn by a patient, thirty years old, who discovered during therapy that the meaning of her life was not only the accumulation of achievements, but rather just being herself. "The meaning of life is being me," said the patient with the joy of a profound epiphany. Throughout the conversation, she drew a circle and added, joyfully, more and more circles. These were, according to her, her "versatile me"—the one that activated her appropriate "me" each time and expressed the connections with other people's "me."

This way, the patient discovered her ability to listen to her own inner voice, to listen to her real needs and to become more aware of what her true "me" really was.

She was able to respond and react to daily situations, and to know how to act and why, without the aggressiveness and criticism that were typical of her previous responses. She received a feeling of satisfaction and joy out of the ability to be "her." In that way, the circles intuitively expressed the process of rediscovery of her identity.

There is indeed a huge excitement when a circle comes into being, the dots within it, when finding the "me" reoccurs and brings inner strength out into the world. This can happen at any age.

D | "A triangle.
Far more interesting than a circle."

"A triangle is an interesting shape."

Triangles with multiple colors and directions.

Merav, a twenty-eight-year-old student, came to therapy with attention deficit disorder. She had difficulty writing papers and preparing for exams, which is why she also had difficulties finishing her degree studies. Her drawings were extremely colorful and she enjoyed mixing colors and achieving so many different shades.

This enabled her to learn about her own rich inner world, a world she managed to express in her drawings. While focusing, she pictured the shape of a triangle, and after the process of focusing, she drew it. Later on, she added many other different triangles to her drawing.

Merav pointed out that she liked the shape of the triangle, because, "It's a shape which is far more interesting than the circle. It has determination, edges, many possibilities for movement and dynamics. The triangle changes its character—whether its tip faces upwards or downwards or whether the edges are equal or different."

Is this a lesson in geometry? No. This is a point of view that differs from person to person. Certain people will be soothed by the round shape, while others might need the change and the dynamics in order to relax.

Out of the different triangles that Merav created, and out of the things she said about her work, it was possible to learn about her need for movement and constant change in her life. As a result, the therapy brought up the following questions: how did this quality contribute to her life—to her different experiences, to her courage, curiosity and joy, and how could her need for dynamics also be harmful, for instance when there was a need to be focused? The multiplicity of the triangle—a shape that can be turned in search for its other side, and the way it's perceived and can be reinterpreted—expressed versatility in life. Merav's love for the triangle teaches us also about her personality: one that contains stability (the base) and determination (the tip), which can aid her when she comes across difficulties. Drawing the triangle, and discussing it, enabled the exploration of expressions such as "interesting" and "dull," and trying to color the "dull" in different colors to see whether it could live side by side with the "interesting" and what might enable her to accept it.

In the session we had after drawing the triangles, Merav spontaneously drew a colorful drawing, and now, along with the colors red, orange green and purple, she also discovered the grey, which was "dull," according to her. The colors managed to combine and live side by side: "dull" with "interesting."

The grey enters. The "dull" lives with the "interesting."

E | The cross that helped in choosing a path. Or even two.

The cross that helped in choosing a path.

Reut, a twenty-seven-year-old woman, finished her Masters and came to me for a single counseling session. Reut was working at the time, progressing in her field of studies and was very successful in her job. She came to me for counseling because she had difficulty deciding what to do next. She was contemplating whether to continue life in the "reasonable" professional course in which she was successful, but was feeling, according to her, unhappy and lifeless, or whether she should take time off from her career, listen to her heart and relocate to a place far up north, where she could find a job in a different field—education and therapy.

During our meeting, after helping her to relax with her eyes closed and to focus on everything happening inside her, Reut felt as though she had no thoughts. A void. This was a new feeling for her, after a long period during which she had been very preoccupied with thoughts. To my question—what does this void look like?—she answered that it was gold and black. It appears that, according to her color choice, in Reut's story the void had a unique and high quality meaning.

During the process of focusing, Reut envisaged a clear, strong line that divided the page in two, representing her own dilemma—the difficulty in choosing between the two different possibilities. After a short silence, Reut envisaged a tree on the left, with a tree house where it is "nice and pleasant." Later, on the right, she saw a black lump with lots of orange and yellow. What she felt, in light of what she pictured in her mind, she described as "dazzling." She was then surprised by her need to draw a horizontal wavy line, a line connecting both sides with the color pink. As she opened her eyes, she drew what she'd envisaged on the paper: the black line she saw that crossed the page into two halves, the house on the tree, the "nice and pleasant" on the left side of the page, representing moving to the north, and the black and orange lump on the right side of the page, representing the choice to stay in the center of the country and pursue her career.

Later on, Reut added the pink, wavy, horizontal line that created a cross. During the conversation, Reut realized that she could bear the oppositions and this conflict represented by the cross and its meeting point. She realized that she could combine the different possibilities, even if not necessarily at the same time, or in the exact same way she'd had in mind. Reut felt as though she now had more courage to fulfill her dreams and listen to her authentic inner voice, to the "voices of her heart." She came out of the session very excited, but also more confident in her own emotions, confident that she could now listen to them and thus direct herself along the path that was right for her for that particular period. After a month, she told me she was moving up north.

F | A cross—
should I climb up, or "go with the flow" and expand?

Lilly, forty years old, intelligent and educated, came to therapy because she felt she was going in circles professionally, and that she had no internal feeling to help her know who and what she wanted. According to her, she wanted to specialize in something, aspiring to achieve a great success, but didn't know in what field. My impression was that for her, climbing up was the essential thing, rather than the content.

In a collage she made, Lilly divided and separated the page in two, creating an upper part and a lower part. In the upper part, she stuck on objects that represented the career path: a ladder, closed drawers piled on each other and more objects. In the lower part, there were objects that expressed creativity, such as a sewing machine, handicraft made out of junk, and more. In her observation, and in the conversation we held after the process of creation, Lilly discovered that, due to the many thoughts that were occupying her mind regarding her career, her creative parts were being left behind, abandoned, lifeless. She called it "the horizontal movement which has ceased." During our conversation, Lilly discovered with much excitement and pain her strong need to be successful, a need that left less space for wider observations or deep connections with her authentic inner world and with her emotions. She discovered a reciprocal relationship between the upwards axis and the expanding axis, and also that they are co-dependent: the vertical axis cannot succeed without the horizontal. This discovery influenced her a lot.

Through her collage work, she realized that her desire and longing to be appreciated and loved were what led to her ambitions, and that her curiosity and authenticity were blocked, along with the ability to motivate herself. With time, this discovery helped Lilly to detach herself from the need to be loved and appreciated as a motivation. She found out how to listen to her unique inner cravings. Much like the creation of an imaginary cross, whose vertical and horizontal lines are balanced, this way all her needs could be met, horizontally and vertically.

For this book, I asked Lilly to create the collage again. According to Lilly, her art work made her understand things and change her manner of thinking. In the beginning, she drew three figures on a bench. According to her own interpretation, the figures represented influential, critical characters from her past, and they represented the blocking and criticism that were holding her back until today. Later, she decided

to cut them off, and that way she detached herself, out of her own initiative, from the blocking figures she had drawn.

In the empty space that remained, she added and glued on drawings of a bicycle and of a sun, as a "source of heat, strength and energy" – her own unique strengths that will give her the ability to move on and fulfill her wishes.

The drawing of the bicycle.

From an obstacle to a stepping stone.

In the session we had after creating the collage, Lilly stated, again and again, the deep influence of this discovery, that her ambitions took a primary place in the way she conducted her life. At the same time, she stated that there was an authentic, inner desire to create growing inside her. "It's as though I've discovered a path … as though a balloon has exploded," and, "like the fantasies of the towers blowing in the air have fallen."

The tree that grew high.

In our process of focusing, Lilly pictured a big pebble, one that has changed from an obstacle that was stuck inside her at the beginning of the process, into a beautiful stone upon which she could lean, and out of which she could draw inspiration. Lilly drew the stone she pictured in her imagination, and then spontaneously added a tree. Lilly stated joyfully: "Now there's a ground (the base and horizontal line) out of which I can grow."

In real life, Lilly started working in a place where, even though she may not have been fulfilling all her abilities and ambitions, she did, surprisingly, find serenity and joy. Here is a poem she wrote:

Height of Grass

Up
Down
I have always aspired
Not right,
Not left
As an arrow spread out
Toward the sun
The warm, pleasant, s
plendid burning

Up
Up
I have always prayed
Not to look
At my own roots
Who do not complement

The cold, the inferior, the
embarrassing
The decayed
Far From the ground
The hard, the painful,
the not hugging

To escape
Up Up
And not feel
To climb
Another floor
To want
To feel
Valuable
Appreciated, considered,
important

Up Up
I have never reached
Down down
The earth was waiting
Hard
Painful
Present
Silently
The grass has height too.

After some months, Lilly received an interesting and challenging job offer. Lilly (and I) had a very clear feeling that the offer didn't arrive around that time by coincidence, but as a result of the confidence she had acquired from the wonderful process she'd been through, and is still going through.

Good things were happening. It appears that her ability to reach new insights and internalize them, and also understand and give meaning to the imbalance between the vertical and horizontal, enabled Lilly to discover what was really right for her at any given moment, while at the same time allowed her creative side to burst out. In fact, Lilly created an imaginary intersection between the horizontal and vertical lines. Instead of being blocked and avoiding action and creation, which was her state in the beginning of this process, she began, without fear and out of pure joy, to allow herself to be "in the height of grass" out of calmness, and freed herself from running after status and from the competitiveness that had characterized her ("Grass has height too.") And here, the grass, which received love and appreciation from her, grew very naturally and of its own will.

Lilly now wishes to pass on this new freedom she has acquired to her own children, in order to free them from the need for achievements and from competitiveness that has nothing to do with their own will. She has learned to accept them the way they are—loved, not disappointing, and evolving in their own independent path. Sometimes, therapy creates a change for many generations to come – vertically, as well as horizontally.

G | The cross—
axis of fantasy and axis of grounding

Sometimes, the artistic process and the changing brush stroke can also express the mutual relationship between height and width. Unusually, Tali, a thirty-year-old interior designer, chose to draw on a rectangular paper facing up. Once she'd finished drawing, during our mutual observation of the work, Tali realized that she'd chosen the extended paper in order to express her own infinite fantasies and imagination, as well as the need to focus on herself and on her own creation. Besides this, she'd become aware of an urge to paint with horizontal brush strokes and to draw a home and a ground, expressing her own need for being grounded, for "sanity," and a need to connect and help the environment. That way, through her creation, Tali discovered her need to be grounded and balanced in light of her endless fantasies. The paper lying in front of her and the horizontal brush strokes enabled her, she felt, to balance her opposing desires and to bear them.

An extended paper and horizontal brush strokes.

H | The cross—
When the "cosmic time" and the "human time" meet one another

Avigail, around 60, has been constantly late for our meetings. With sadness, she admitted that she has a tendency to be late everywhere she goes. While drawing, she started crying. When she had finished drawing, she said that drawing made her realize how time had stopped for her somewhere around the traumatic childhood experience of her father's death. She felt that she remained with him somewhere in the cosmic and infinite time, and this had created a sense of dizziness and blurriness and caused her to lose her sense of time.

She continued to describe the two different timelines in which she carried herself, and named them "cosmic time" and "human time." She could not combine the two of them and "cosmic time" always won over "human time". At the beginning of the drawing process, she drew a watch where the head was, representing rational time, or "human" time, a timeline that comes from the head with no emotional connection. As she continued to draw, she added another circle and marked a horizontal line underneath the watch. While looking at the drawing, she added the vertical line, (the "me" standing on its feet—as described in Chapter 4/C- p. 53-58 "The cross") going downward. Unknowingly, it seems as though she had connected the sky with the earth, the cosmic, and the real.

At the end of the process, she added the ground at the bottom of the page. She became more and more excited about discovering her own "grounding" and connecting to reality. The horizontal and vertical lines, which met at the center of the page, created the cross which connected the contrasts of the split timelines, the cosmic, and the real that accompanied her. The memories of the past that she had expressed (the trauma and infinite cosmic time) and the encounter with the present (dealing with the current time through understanding her tendency of arriving late and the process of drawing itself) and the future (her desire to change) could come to terms with one another. Her perception of time was accompanied by depth and insight.

"When 'cosmic time' and 'human time' meet one another."

The week after, she arrived at our session on time for the first time since she began therapy, and said, "When I look at the stable and balanced cross, I feel and understand how strong I am, and that it is so different from perceiving myself as weak."

I | "From the circle to my own house."

This example describes the process of emotional development during therapy, as it appears in the drawings of a 30-year-old woman. Through this, we can see how this has a resemblance to the chronological development in children's drawings.

Sheli, around 30 years old, came to therapy to gain the strength and the courage to change her life trajectory from work in the technology industry to the field of design. She approached the drawing process with a sense of lightness and freedom, not needing any instructions during the sessions. Slowly, through the therapeutic process, I noticed how her drawings developed from week to week. The changes in her drawings occurred in a similar pattern to the order of development that appears in children's drawings. The contents and the graphical abilities were of course more sophisticated and complex than those of children, but the sequence of development and the meaning of the shapes' order of appearance was similar. (See p. 159, p. 170-171)

Similar to the development of children's drawings, she began by drawing a circle, representing the construction of the "me" discovering its own ability to separate from the "other" and to become independent. Later, horns appeared, extruding from the circle as an expression of the ability to publicize the inner world, of reaching out, and the desire to examine one's relationship with the outer world. A picture of a house then appeared, which represents, much like in children's drawings, stability and unification.

In one of her first drawings, Sheli drew a **whole circle**, in which the characters of a mother and a son had merged.

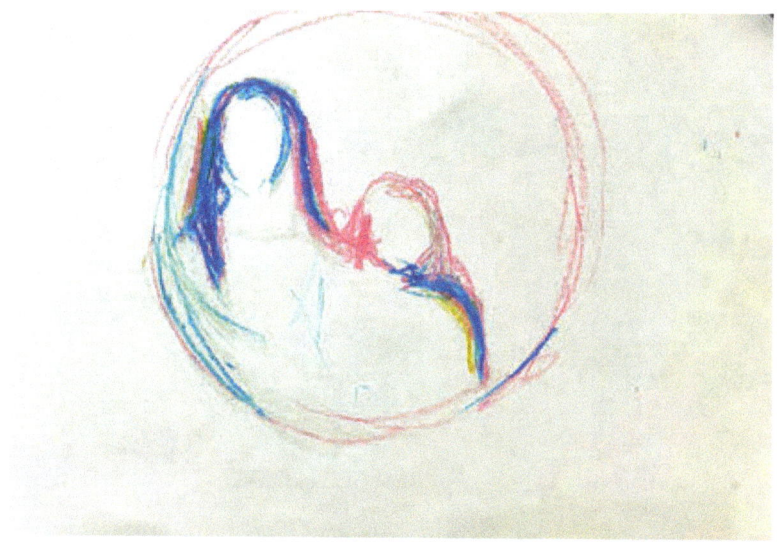

„A circle with a merging mother and son."

After a few weeks, Sheli started **separating the circles**, with one common center in the middle. One circle represented her son and the other represented her—the mother. Separating the circle represents the process of separation. Sheli's work demonstrates how the mother also has an active role in the process of separation—not only is the child separating from his mother, the mother is also separating from her son. In one of our sessions, Sheli started drawing herself using a smaller circle, but slowly during the session, while observing, she enlarged the circle. In doing so, she enlarged her presence in the relationship.

The process of separation between mother and son

The next circle drawn by Sheli a few weeks later was full and rich and contained the shape of the **cross**. Sheli drew one hinge vertically, marked by the standing figure, and the second hinge as a horizontal line dividing the "upper" part from the "lower.". The figure stands at the meeting point of the two hinges and seems as though it is watching the world. Sheli stated while observing the drawing that there is movement going in both directions. It is simultaneously going up towards the sun and the wind, and down toward gravity and the earth—represented by the tree in the drawing.

The circle representing the "me" in this drawing seems rich, complex, and balanced. It can contain the contrasts of up and down, earth and ground.

"A rich inner world and the formed cross"

A week later, Sheli started working on her ability to be present with a re-
laxing empty circle, which stands on its own and is not dependent on the
other (the green contour representing the circle). According to her, in this
stage, she is capable of creating. This is a void representing strength and
space where she can create.

That way she can play, enjoy and move between the two different states
she has drawn. The full circle (the above painting) and the empty circle (the
next painting) are two states in the process of recharging and emptying.
She moves between two different states that need one another, representing
her ability to find the way to become full and creative each time.

The powerful void and the space of creation

After Sheli drew and expressed her sense of abundance inside the circle, and the way she charges and fills it up, she drew another **circle with horns** or spikes protruding out towards the world, toward the "other." That way, she can examine how she appears to the outer world as well as her relationship with the "other." The gap was manifested in the two different colors she had chosen: the red she chose for the inside, "love and warmth" according to her, and the green she chose for the horns, reaching outside the world with their sharp edges (at least some of them).

A circle with horns reaching out to the world

Sheli had realized, through observing the drawing, that she did not express truly how she felt inside. For her message to be accepted and understood, she needed to express her feelings less angrily, in a warmer and more loving way. A week later, Sheli drew a figure, with which she continued to work on the gaps between her outer and inner world.

As the process continued, Sheli drew colorful rectangles spontaneously, spread across the paper, representing her being competent, practical, and effective. Next, she added grey stripes going downwards and said, "One needs to balance the matter and the spirit to do and create." By adding the grey vertical stripes, she created an experience similar to the drawing of the cross, the possibility of containing and holding contrasts.

"The cross-balance between matter and spirit."

A week later, Sheli continued drawing a **house that was being constructed**. A house with a triangular roof ("How to build a house" Chapter 6, p.9) and a tree next to it, representing the growing attention to her environment. Constructing the house, as she said, marked the beginning of the construction of her new career, the one she asked for from within herself, which more closely resembled her real "me." Her dream was forming a shape and was now being manifested as a house.

The dream formulated as a house

Shortly before the end of the therapeutic process, Sheli drew a tree representing her vision. While observing her drawing, she said, "This is my vision and how I want to be, with balanced thoughts and strong roots, so strong I don't need to give them much thought. I want the stem clear and present, which means my position is clear and present. I want my environment to be fertile and to enable me to fulfill my existing potential."

"The tree of my vision, or how I want to be."

In our last session, Sheli drew a tree with roots, stronger, richer, more grounded, its stem thickening, its roots deepening into the ground, and its branches reaching toward the sky. According to her, the tree in the drawing described her feelings and the way she had matured during these months of therapy, and how her vision became closer to reality.

A tree that is expanding and progressing—the vision is close to becoming real

Looking back at the progression of drawings, one can see Sheli had undergone a clear and evolving process. This process moved from the initial use of simple, almost childish shapes to the expression of more complex, rich shapes with a deeper and wider perspective, expressing the process of her own personal and professional growth.

J | The gaze that influenced a life story—from a feeling of missing out to a feeling of acceptance

Erna, fifty years old, came to therapy because of a feeling that she'd missed out on something in her life, although, in reality, she had built a successful career. In our meetings, she found it important to make her drawings pretty and pleasing. The first drawings were very controlled, with clear boundaries, out of an attempt not to reveal any emotions or weaknesses. Maybe, that way, she felt she could be appreciated and loved.

Over time, Erna learned to recognize her need to create a "beautiful drawing" and let go of it, be more authentic and accept herself the way she was, with her weaknesses. Our conversations that accompanied the process were about her childhood, revealing how critical her parents had been, their high expectations of her, and their inability to see her and accept her the way she was. The experience of her parents judging and critical gaze influenced her and turned her into a critical adult, one who lives life with a feeling of missing out.

In the process of therapy, Erna had a "corrective experience" through the support and acceptance of the therapist, and through her ability to accept her drawings the way they were, even when the shapes were fluid or less "pretty" and controlled. This new acceptance, along with the conversations we held and the insights we reached during our sessions, enabled her to go through a gradual process of letting go of the expectations and criticism that were part of her childhood experience.

The process Erna went through was also visible in the changes in her drawings. Gradually, she started drawing more and more out of an inner, authentic and spontaneous experience, and not to please. Paradoxically, the drawings became prettier in her eyes.

And indeed, in the more authentic of her drawings in which her "true self" appeared, different, deeper qualities of beauty were evident. At the end of the therapy process, involving many conversations and drawings, Erna was able to come to terms with the course of her career, with love and acceptance – and, even though it was different from what she had envisioned, she felt happy, and felt as though she was fulfilling her wishes and going in the right direction.

Decorating with yellow and white to appease.

Beginning to shed off the defenses and the decorations.

**Continuing to shed off the defenses and the decorations.
She finds the drawing pretty.**

**An integration of all the colors—is an authentic drawing, drawn from
within and not in order to appease.**

Another drawing that was created as an authentic, personal expression.

Out of these examples and others, we can see that there is a fundamental resemblance in dealing with children's and adult's drawings. The parallel between the processes of construction of the different shapes and their emotional meaning can occur at any given age. As time went by, I noticed that I had formed a new manner of "observing": even when patients had not yet drawn anything, or spoken about themselves verbally, I began to picture in my mind a doodle, a circle, a cross or horns, as though they were drawn above their heads. I found myself being aided by the shapes that appeared in my mind in order to understand the stage at which the patients had come to therapy.

A twenty-seven-year-old guy, a successful hi-tech employee who was looking for a change, came to consult with me. He told me he was trying to decide between the temptation of working in a fixed, well-paid job, and the possibility of working in something creative and more emotionally rewarding, but which paid less. And there I was, picturing the doodle above his head. I could see his confusion, and simultaneously I could see a cross, telling me that he was confident and determined, and that the two opposing directions of the search and the wondering and the soul-searching could meet in the future. When I described to him the shapes I could "see" above his head and explained their meanings to him, he understood and felt calmed. He experienced this as an illustration of his own emotions. For me, this has become another way of evaluating and studying the emotional state the person is in.

Here is a small reminder of the stages of drawings and their emotion meanings:

Doodling: pace, primality, vitality, spontaneity—or searching, restlessness and anxiety.

Circle: an experience of forming a self, separateness, reciprocal relations of interior and exterior, "me" versus "not-me," softness, flow, binding.

A dot inside the circle: there is something living inside of me.

Horns: one can go out—a feeling of growth.

Cross: the ability to bear opposition, and an inner world that is complex; searching for direction in life, ambitions, going horizontally or vertically… which direction is desirable and which one attainable… what is the extent to which the directions are balanced, and whether it might be right and possible to combine the different directions and possibilities.

Triangle: the presence of boundaries and a base, assertiveness, planning, dynamics, and dealing with triangular relationships.

Chapter Eleven

"Please Do Not Disturb—I'm drawing"
Your toolbox (and some tips, too)

"Do not disturb?"

"A toolbox?"

These terms are, indeed, rather complex and evasive. How can one be both present and active without interfering?

Winnicott has described the therapist (and perhaps also the parent) who knows too much, as one who "steals" creativity away from his patients (or his children).

We're talking here about being a liberating presence, one which is devoid of our usual observation, a presence in which we are watching what's happening with curiosity and patience, while leaving any previous knowledge behind.

Try to listen with your eyes to what you're seeing without being pushy; let the process evolve on its own in a natural way. Let yourself loose and observe from your heart, with honesty and seriousness. Try to walk in the child's shoes, contemplate his emotions and the contents of his work and let go, if only for a short while, of any expectations that you may come across.

That way, you will respect the child's uniqueness, and enable him to take the lead. A warm and enabling environment will be created, his own private space, one that will allow him to be himself—one that supports his selfhood, his inner life, his imagination and his art works.

Being present while listening silently is an action perceived as passive, but actually, it's an active action that requires a huge amount of effort and intention. When we connect with the child in the correct manner, we enable him to be trusting, to become more dedicated to the experience, and to develop into a creative, brave and resourceful adult.

The psychoanalyst, Masud Khan, compares this idea to a field that is openly waiting to be sown, a kind of waking silence. That is also what Marion Milner (1900-1998), a British psychoanalyst who has done a lot of research on creativity and analysis, writes in her book *The Suppressed Madness of Sane Men*:

> *"And then I asked—can we summarize what the will has to do? It seemed that it certainly has to wait in very active present mindedness and be content with being a frame holding the empty space for something new to emerge, something that has never been before."*

A quiet and serious observation of the child as he creates can give him the feeling that what he's doing is right and good. Responses should be given when the child asks for them, (or when you want or need to say something). They should be objective, not regarding the content and especially not regarding the quality, but simply on what you are seeing:

"You have lots of colors here."
"What a long line… rolling… a new line."
"You're such an inventor of lines… shapes…. dots… colors"
"I see you really drew what you were feeling today."

Your honest response is very meaningful to him, even if it's just in your look. Try not to distract him with questions and requests, not to judge, direct or fix anything. There's no "right" and "wrong" in personal expression. Try not to think of achievements, but rather the space given to the expression of the different emotions and the joy in this process. Try to be patient as possible (this isn't easy) as the change and development will occur gradually and at the right pace, a pace that comes from within. The interesting absurdity is that the joy, even if it is doodled, repetitive or vague, is the biggest promoter. Experimenting and making mistakes are the best ways of learning.

Freeing oneself from an ideal perception of a "product" is the real freedom, one which will enable and give the courage, to invent and create new ideas.

So take it slowly. Simply enjoy, and let them see it!

Here are some tips for creating an encouraging, free, trusting and authentic environment:

How can we turn the blank page into an inviting playground?

A | Place

If there's a place in the house that you can allow to get dirty without being concerned, it would be excellent for your child's experimenting. You could designate a wall for it: hang up a plywood or cork board, an easel, or some corrugated plastic sheet, (perhaps you can also protect the floor). Drawing standing up allows the body to be free and represents the horizontal direction of the posture and the space of reality of being either up or down, heads and feet, as well as a more open space for the drawing hands.

A freestyle drawing that was done standing up.

If it isn't possible to paint against a wall, you could use a protected floor space, or a table, one you don't mind getting dirty and that can be easily cleaned if necessary. The paper that will serve for the artwork can be taped down to stop it from moving, to provide a safe and satisfying area to work in. It's important to make the child feel as though the place where he's working is safe, to make it as enabling as possible.

B | Material

Allow the toddler to experiment with painting on paper in different sizes. It's also useful to expose him to pages bigger than the standard A4. Half a sheet, or even a sheet, will be challenging. A board 50x60 cm would be great. The size opens up and allows space for movement. If the child is frustrated by the size, go back to the size he's used to, until he feels like experimenting again. Be aware of his frustration or enthusiasm.

Encourage the use of gouache paints, which are suitable for using with water, encourage the flow and freedom, and enable mixing and creating new shades of color. You shouldn't be afraid of mixing, even if sometimes it may just look like mud. This is a wonderful experience in exploring one's many emotions, the diversity of the world, and the ability to be flexible to the many possibilities and solutions in life.

C | Diversity

Try to let the child paint on anything that isn't standard paper, and maybe not even use a standard brush. They can paint on a paper soaked with water, on colorful paper, plates, cups, boxes, balloons, clothes, brick walls in the yard. They can use a stick, a leaf from outside, or yarn as a brush to dip inside the paint… as far as the imagination goes. Sometimes the child may feel more safe and free of expectations in that manner. In this way, unexpected creative ideas could arise in him. If these alternatives aren't possible, give him marker pens or oil crayons, and the possibility to create with joy—because that's the main thing.

Chapter Twelve

"Take a look at the drawing: it's a body"
Drawing as an expression of the body

> *"The artist is the hand which plays, touching one key or another, to cause vibration in the soul."*
> W. Kandinsky—"concerning the spiritual in art"

In this chapter, I will describe how the physical body, its sensations, and its emotional image are present in drawings, and how they manifest themselves within various ways—be they abstract or naturalistic, conscious or subconscious.

First, connection manifests in different ways in the process of creation—a process that uses the 'pure' physical body, the observing eyes, the touch of the drawing hands and, at times, even the creator's body itself (see the drawings of Ram Samucha,p.45). This connection is also expressed in the physical and emotional reactions that accompany the drawing and change upon viewing it. A deepening breath, a heart expanding, a voice growing louder, or eyes widening and brightening. Smiles, laughter, happiness, consolation, satisfaction, pain, fear, wonder, sadness, and sometimes even tears—all of these might appear at the sight of a drawing.

The unique subject explored throughout this chapter is that of the 'imprinted' body—the body that manifests itself by hiding in the drawing, without the creator's conscious intention.

Drawings created spontaneously with no instructions—the way I normally work in a therapy session—whether realistic (such as houses, figures, and trees), abstract, planned or spontaneous, all hold an affinity to the physical body of the person who drew them and to his subjective body experience.

I have asked patients ranging from young children to adults what they see in their drawings, particularly the abstract ones, and which body part they have drawn (for my research purposes).

I was surprised by how quickly, naturally, and firmly they could answer which body part is reflected in their drawings. Every patient reacts in a unique and individual way, each from their own perspective.

Gali

Gali, around 30 years old, was yearning for a career change but was too afraid of actually executing this change. When I asked her after she finished painting, "Which body part did you draw?" she looked at the drawing and answered, "This is the belly when it gets excited."

When she looked at the drawing once again, she said, surprised, "I feel as though my belly is aching even now as I look at the drawing."

Gali: "This is the belly when it gets excited."

Leah

In her seventies, Leah was impressed by the diverse landscapes she saw in the abstract drawing that she had created, and told me it portrayed "water, mountains, and a forest."

When I asked her which part of her body the drawing represents, she answered that it represents the head and then continued with a satisfied smile, "a head that has everything." A statement that reflected her sense of abundance.

Leah: "This is the head that has everything."

Noa

At 40, Noa had come to therapy to try to become more flexible, forgiving, and less critical towards herself and others. As she was observing the abstract drawing that she had spontaneously drawn, she wondered aloud, "Why are there so many eyes here?"

When I asked, "What eyes?" she responded clearly and quickly, "The ones inside the light blue stripe in the middle of the page." The numerous eyes that she saw in the drawing might represent her sensitivity to how others might perceive her and her criticism of herself and others.

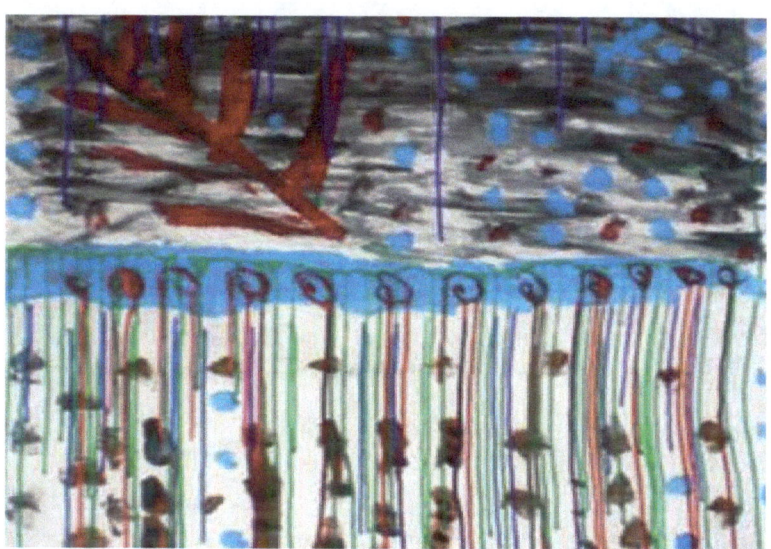

Noa: "Why are there so many eyes here?"

Ron

Ron, a 6-year-old, saw a belly reflected in his drawing. While observing the drawing, he said that it (the belly) has life, and that is why he will never die.

Ron: "The belly has life, and that is why I will never die."

One can see from these examples how natural it was for patients to visualise and connect to how each drawing represented their own bodies.

The variety and specificity of body parts seen by patients in their drawings show how meaningful and sensitive these body parts are perceived to be, and what a unique and intimate connection there is between the creator and their body.

The head, the eyes, and the belly reflected and imprinted in these patients' drawings are related to emotions and sensations such as pain, happiness, memory, conflict, and excitement.

This theme of the body and its image is complex. On one hand, there is a **concrete external** body, revealed and exposed with clear contours (the skin) including body parts such as the face, the hands, and the legs. On the other hand, there is a **concrete internal** body, including body parts such as the heart, the lungs, and the stomach.

Beyond these approaches to the concept of body, there is also a **subjective approach**, which deals with both the **internal and the external body**. This is constructed of feelings, thoughts, sensations, memories, imagination, images, and fantasy. With drawing, one can express the experience of their body with its many different layers and also describe what is **felt but is left unseen**.

For example, 11-year-old Shiri, who was drawing spontaneously with gouache, named her drawing "**Body X-Ray.**" Through the use of different shapes and colors, she was able to represent her interpretation and perception of invisible parts of her body.

Daphne

Another example of different aspects of the body experience is the work of twenty-year-old Daphne, a work in which the **concrete and imaginary body intertwine.**

The external contour, the shape and placement of the lungs and the ribs remind us of the real body, but inside the contour, the heart is located in the middle, in an imaginary place. "The heart I drew seems like a green shield, and I see it is much like the green circle surrounding the body, which is also there to protect it," she said, impressed, while observing the drawing. Daphne chose colors unrepresentative of the actual colors of the body. She selected colors according to her imagination and emotion, and through shape and colour demonstrated a unique expression to the subjective emotional experience of a body that is yearning for protection.

Daphne: a drawing with the concrete and imaginary body intertwined.

Rachel

An example of a sensory and bodily drawing experience can be found in the drawing of Rachel, 50, who drew spontaneously without a brush, eyes closed.

Rachel was invested fully in the experience, subjected to the **sensation** of the color and its soft **touch on her hand**. As she opened her eyes, she was greeted by the shape of a cross with a horizontal and a vertical hinge. "The meeting point of these hinges and the thing that connects them to each other seems like a **heart**," she said excitedly.

Rachel found comfort in the fact that she had formed a heart—a heart that assembles and connects all of her contradicting and complex emotions.

This observation gave her a pleasant, safe feeling of gathering and integration.

Looking again at the drawing, Rachel saw it as if it were a tree, representing her spiritual and physical self.

Rachel: "The meeting point of these hinges looks like a heart."

The analyst Susan Bach, who has explored the expression of the body in drawings, wrote in her book "Life Paints Its Own Span" (1990), that in addition to the mental state reflecting itself in the drawing, the physical and bodily state also reflect in colors and shapes.

According to Bach, one can, in freestyle drawings, see a present physical condition (such as diseases), a physical condition from the past, and even a future body state such as pregnancy, unknown even to the drawer herself.

The physical sensations and their meanings can be expressed in different parts of the drawing. Observations can use physiological descriptors such as density and lightness, big and small, narrow and space-consuming, soft and hard, light and heavy. For example, many drawings exhibit heaviness in the lower part of the paper. They are condensed and full of color and shapes, in a way that could be a sign of grounding, heaviness, or concrete pain in the legs.

Sometimes, one can see drawings full and condensed in the upper part of the paper, using colors or contents that may express heaviness, unclarity, a busy mind, or an overload of thoughts. The use of light and delicate colors, imagery like butterflies or fairies, or a light breeze blowing in the upper part of the drawing can be evidence of dealing with the spiritual and not the material, or of happiness and lightness.

The typical order of development in children's drawings, as described in the previous chapters, goes from doodling to forming a figure, or—as sometimes occurs in the therapeutic process—from drawing a figure to drawing a freestyled, abstract drawing. This order marks the movement of feelings and thoughts, the experience of the self, and the changing body image of the one who's drawing as well as their changing relationships with space, the "other" and with their environment.

Parameters such as size, placement, heaviness and lightness, the thickness of boundaries, and colors that stand out as opposed to hidden ones (such as white on white paper) that will change during the process; all represent change and development.

The significance of the relationship between body, space, and the environment depicted by drawing is evidenced in the therapeutic process that Hagit, a 30-year-old woman, went through. Hagit drew a sun with sunbeams all over the paper. At first, she said she did not like the beams because they seemed "too aggressive." After observation and a talk during our session, this feeling changed, and she wanted to put more emphasis on the beams. She felt as though she in fact did want this power.

Hagit was happy with the process and the change she underwent during the session. She was able to feel as though she could take more space and enlarge her presence in the world. In this way, she strengthened her own self-image and her body image.

Drawing is unique because it enables the creator (of all ages), whether consciously or unconsciously, to express their experiences of both the subjective and the objective body, of both the hidden and the exposed, as well as the physical and the metaphysical experience. Drawing is a symbolic container of thoughts and emotions, ones that are impossible to discover through observation alone. **Colors and shapes marked on the paper hold within them the intimate existential depth of the body.** One can look at it as a unique mirror in which one can see the body and the spirit in all their different aspects.

Observing one's drawing has a meaningful and important part in the construction of the "me" and the body image. The gaze is subjective and complex, accompanied by the imagination and emotions (of both the observer and observed).

Marion Milner writes in her book "On Not Being Able to Paint" (1957) that there is no such thing as an objective gaze. She states that the gaze cannot stand on its own. It is always wrapped in emotion and there is no such thing as an objective reality. In "Concerning the Spiritual in Art" (1977), Kandinsky too demonstrates how colors can be either rough, spiky, hard, or soft. He compares the observation of a drawing to the tasting of high quality or sophisticated food. Such is the gaze accompanying the parent, the therapist, and the child's supportive environment. It is a **beneficial gaze**, one that is full of attention and sensitivity to the assimilated and "**live**" **body** that appears in the drawing, and will contribute to the drawer's confidence to be themselves. It is also what would aid in a healthy construction of body image, and what will ensure this image is built with confidence and love.

It seems as though the creator is more attentive to their body and emotions through drawing than what they are consciously aware of. Let's find a way to be, with our own gazes, like an attentive and wrapping sun to every creator whose drawing we observe.

Chapter Thirteen

An activity for keepsake

The French poet, Baudelaire, claimed that children see everything as new. According to him, there is nothing in this world that resembles what we call "inspiration" more than the joy with which a child perceives shapes and colors.

The following pages are for you to paste in any paintings, doodles and drawings by your child—or for him to draw directly on these designated pages. You can document his transition from doodling to drawing a circle, a figure, and so on. That way, you can keep the drawings and enjoy the journey your child has made—his transition from doodling to drawing a figure. a reflection of your child's process of growing up will be documented in these changing and evolving drawings.

When he's all grown up, your child's joy at seeing these pages will be huge! Through them he can access in a unique way another piece of information about himself and his childhood, realize the extent of your love for him, and see that he was so important to you that you took the trouble to keep his artwork in this way. If you also feel like doodling—go for it!

A small reminder before the activity:

Doodling: a motor stage (Ages one to three)

Congratulations! The circle is born out of the doodle. (Ages three to four)

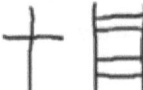

Crosses and ladders: the world consists of oppositions. Not simple anymore, but interesting. (Ages three to four)

There is a dot: something alive and whole within me. The "me" is now confident enough to come out to the world. (Ages three to four)

A circle with horns on it: coming out into the world.

A complex triangle: we already have three lines. It's good to have a base. (Age four.)

I can already draw a figure and a house. (Ages four to five)

Colors: such fun!

The universality of the order of development of the drawings, along with the uniqueness and the pace of each drawing, create the feeling that there is beauty and order to the world, and it creates a lot of enthusiasm, doesn't it?

Now you can enjoy your child's private collection, and draw here with joy.

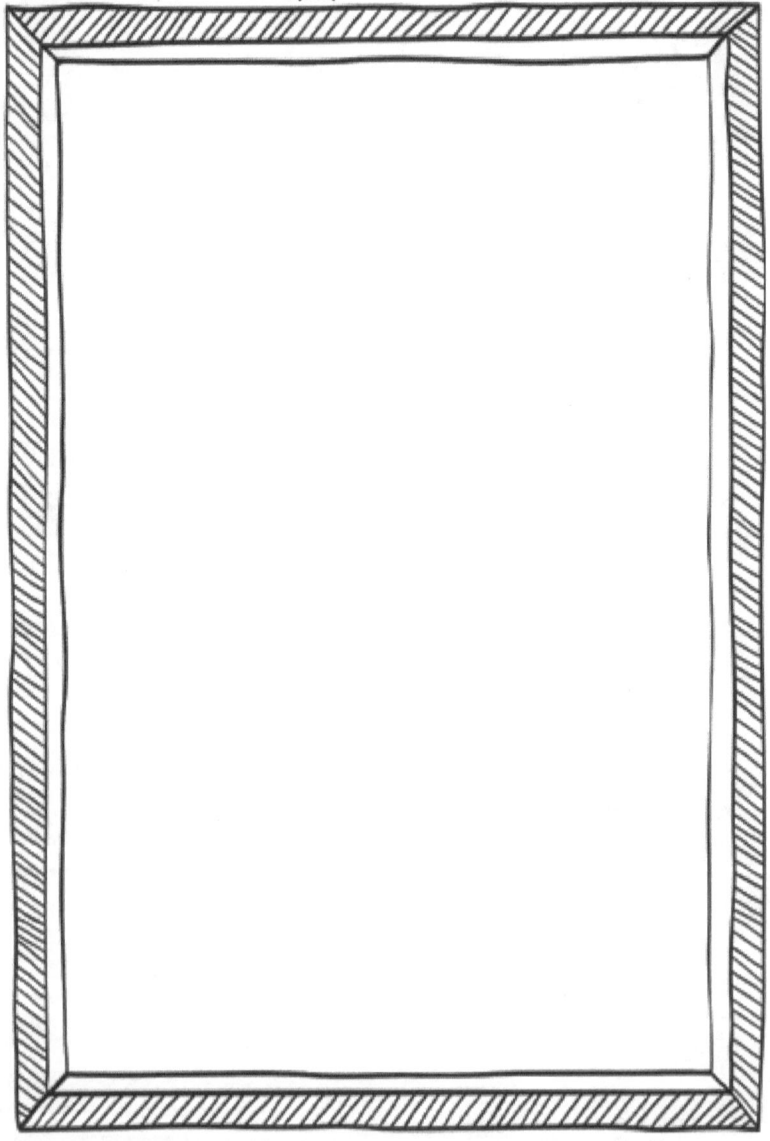

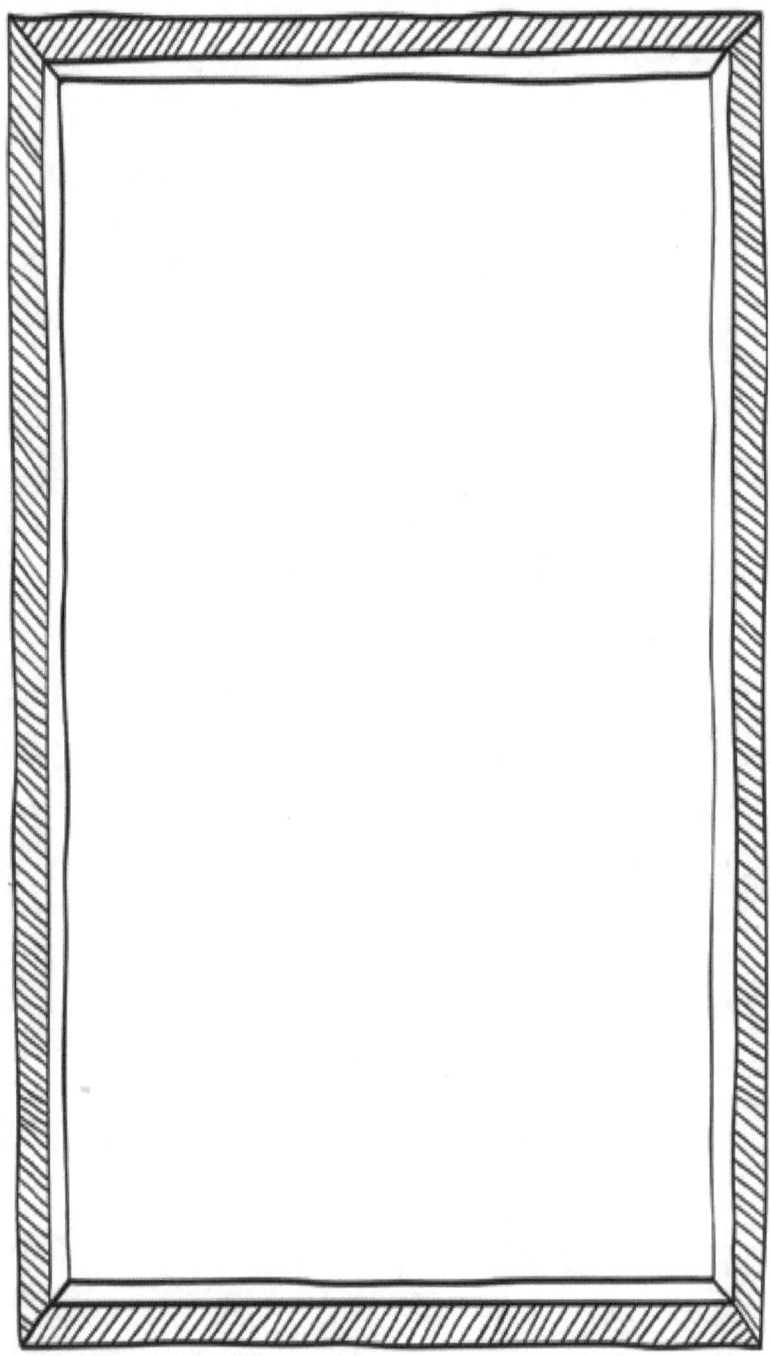

Thanks

When I think of all the people who have inspired new and nurturing feelings within me that have aided me in the writing of this book, a big smile and an image of a warm sun appears.

Thanks to my wonderful friends, who have been so patient, giving and wise—each has contributed out of her own skills and out of her own unique personality: Racheli Dar-Rosenfeld, Galila Oren, Ziona Frenkel, Chana Soker Shvager, Yehudit Triest, Adva Oved Golani, Dana Salmon and Tamar Bassan. You are all written here as one group, but each one of you is unique, and a special place is held for you in my heart.

Thanks to Ofer Gol, a dear friend whom I was lucky enough to get to know, through the inspiration of our mutual love for books in the inspirational project "Book surfing," for his generous and kind support in my search for the right combination and balance of mind and matter, and for him being both a marketing man and a man of letters.

Thanks to Chana Kalderon, editor and journalist of many years experience, who encouraged me while the book was still in its early stages and gave me very wise and important advice.

Thanks to my dear patients, who have trusted me and allowed me to be a part of their journey, and to share it. Thanks to the parents of the children who have acknowledged the importance of the book and its meaning, and contributed their children's drawings; and to Nili Naor, who kept the booklet that was given to her by her fellow first graders—and gave it to me.

Thanks to the wonderful artists Ram Samucha, Yael Balaban and Tamar Doborovski, who have allowed me to share and combine their work in this book, and also to Prof. Itamar Procaccia, who let me use artwork from his Japanese collection. These breathtaking creations have made a great contribution to the beauty of the book and to the depth of the insights that were embedded in it regarding art. It is an honor.

Thanks to the professional staff whose work has required lots of dedication and patience: Miriam Kutz for her support and encouragement and professionalism. Miriam has managed to collate the written pieces and helped them to become an accurate whole. Her contribution to the book is huge.

Thanks to Chen Yaka Shomron for her significant contribution to the concept design.

Thanks to Avi Levi for the professionalism and patience that were required to photograph and process both, the original drawings and the ones sent over the internet.

Thanks to Roni Bogin—who has translated the book in a very professional manner, with great attendance to the book's "music", and with a profound understanding of its spirit and its professional contact.

Thanks to Yael and Karen from "Notssa publishing" for the dedication and the professional approach, and also for the pleasant and fertilizing dialogue we have established throughout the publishing process.

The book is dedicated with love

To my dear parents, Zipora and Norman, who helped me to become "me."

To my beloved children—Roni, Ben and Tom, without them, the book would not have been born.

To my dear friends—Miki Shilo and Mali Reichmen, RIP—whose inspiration is always with me.

Bibliography

References and quotes that have influenced the writing of this book with
their content and spirit

1. Bach, S. (1990). "Life Paints its own Span". Daimon Verlag publishing.
   Switzerland
2. Ballas, G. (1996). *Colour in Modern Painting, Theory and Practice*. La-
   or Publishing. Israel.Translated by Roni Bogin. pp.168-182; 109-117;
   123-135
3. Baudelaire, C. (1863). *Le peintre de la vie modern*.
4. Betansky, M. (1995) *What do you See? Phenomenlogy of therapeutic art
   expression*. Jessica kingsley Londonpenns publishers.
5. Da Vinci, L. (2008). *Leonardo da Vinci's Note-books*. Oxford University
   Press. p.7.
6. Bogin M. (2010). *Observing the Speaking Body*. published by The Hebrew Psychology Website.
7. Gendlin, E. T. (1981). *Focusing*. Bantam Doubleday Dell Publishing
   Group.
8. Goldberg L. (1973). *On Three Things the World Stands*. Hakibutz Ha-
   meuchad—Sifriat Poalim Publishing Group. Translated by Roni Bogin.
9. Jung, C. G. (1959). *The Archetypes and the Collective Unconscious*. Pa-
   theon, New York.
10. Kandinsky, W. (1977). *Concerning the Spiritual in Art*. Dover Publisi-
    ons, London. p. 35-36, 38.
11. Kellogg, R. (1969). *Analyzing Children's Art*. Mayfield Pub Co.
12. Khans, M. (1989). *Hidden Selves: Between theory and practice in psy-
    choanalysis*. Masterfield Library. London.
13. Klee, P., Spiller J. (ed). (1961). *Paul Klee Notebooks, The Thinking Eye*.
    Lund Humphries, London.
14. Klee, F. (ed). (1964). *The Diaries of Paul Klee, 1898-1918*. University of
    California Press, Berkley and Los Angeles.
15. Kohut, H. (1985). *Self Psychology and the Humanities*. Charles B. Stro-
    zier and Elizabeth Kohut.
16. Lacan, J. (1982). *Écrits*. W.W. Norton & Company.
17. Livio, M. (2002). *The Golden Ratio*. Broadway Publishing Group (Ran-
    dom House). New York.
18. Lowenfeld,V. Britten W.L. (1987). *Creative and Mental Growth*. Mac-
    milian Publishing Company.

19. Malchiodi, C. A. (1998). *Understanding Children's Drawings.* Guilford Press. N.Y.-London
20. Milner, M. (1988). *The Suppressed Madness of Sane Men.* Routledge. London. P.79.
21. Milner, M. (1957). *On not being able to paint.* International Universities Press, INC
22. Perec, G. (1974). *Espèces d'espaces.* Galilée. Paris. Pp. 21-23.
23. Scharfstein, B. A. (2006). *Spontaneity in Art.* Am Oved books. Israel. Translated by Roni Bogin
24. Scharfstein, B. A. (2007). *Birds, Elephants, Apes and Children.* Am Oved books and Xargol books. Israel. Translated by Roni Bogin.
25. Stern, A., Lindbergh, P., & Lindbergh, P. (2005). *Heureux. Comme Un Enfant Qui Peint.* Du Rocher.
26. Strauss, M. (1978). *Understanding Children's Drawings.* Rudolf Steiner Press, London.
27. Tustin, F. (1986). *Autistic Barriers in Neurotic Patience.* Karnac Books.
28. Tustin, F. (1981). *Autistic States in Children.* Routledge. P.158
29. Winnicott, D.W. (2005). *Playing and Reality.* Routledge.

Art pieces

1. Balaban,Y. (2010). *Target Game of Dreams.* Touches and pyrograph on mazonite.
2. Balaban,Y. (2014). *Dressed man.* Ink on paper.
3. Dubrosky,T. (2014). *Creation Series,* Mixed media on paper
4. Klee, P. (1930). *Ad Marginem.*
5. Samocha, R. (2009). *New Born.* Drawing performance with colour pencil, photo by Ram Samocha.
6. Samocha, R. (2015). Toping. *Drawing performance with silicon,* photo by Marco Berardi
7. *At the Tip of a Brush, Clouds and Wind* (2015) The Wilfrid Israel Museum of Asian. Japanese paintings from the collection of Prof. Itamar Procaccia.

Zeitfracht Medien GmbH
Ferdinand-Jühlke-Straße 7
99095 Erfurt, Deutschland
produktsicherheit@kolibri360.de